Get INVOLVED!

American Edition

2

Student's Book

with Digital Student's Book

Gill Holley Kate Pickering

Get INVOLVED! American Edition

Collaborative projects

Collaborate with your classmates to develop your problem-solving skills in the WDYT? projects. Become an expert on a topic and get involved with others in your class.

WDYT?
(What do you think?)

Real-world content

Learn about culture while you learn English. *Get Involved! American Edition* is full of real-world content, so go online and learn more about the people, events and places in the book.

Super skills

Get Involved! American Edition helps develop your critical thinking, collaboration, creativity and communication skills, which are essential for life in the 21st century.

COLLABORATION

CRITICAL THINKING

COMMUNICATION

CREATIVITY

Building skills for the real world

Social and emotional learning

Get Involved! American Edition helps you develop strategies to deal with social situations and gives you the vocabulary you need to discuss emotions that you or others experience.

Five reasons why stepping out of your comfort zone is good for you

Media-rich content

Get Involved! American Edition videos help you with critical thinking, communication and project presentations and improve your video literacy skills. Access On-the-Go Practice on your phone through the Macmillan Student's App and improve your English with gamified content.

Inclusive classroom

Show your strengths and talents by putting your investigative skills and logic to the test with *Get Involved! American Edition* Brain teasers. Learn at your own pace with reinforcement and challenge activities in the Grammar bootcamp and graded Workbook activities.

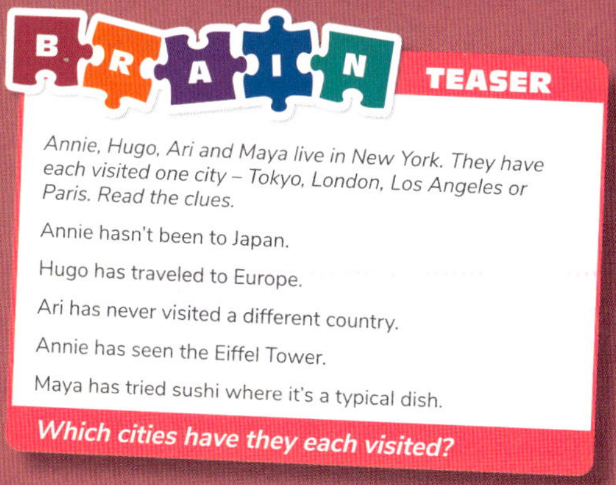

BRAIN TEASER

Annie, Hugo, Ari and Maya live in New York. They have each visited one city – Tokyo, London, Los Angeles or Paris. Read the clues.

Annie hasn't been to Japan.

Hugo has traveled to Europe.

Ari has never visited a different country.

Annie has seen the Eiffel Tower.

Maya has tried sushi where it's a typical dish.

Which cities have they each visited?

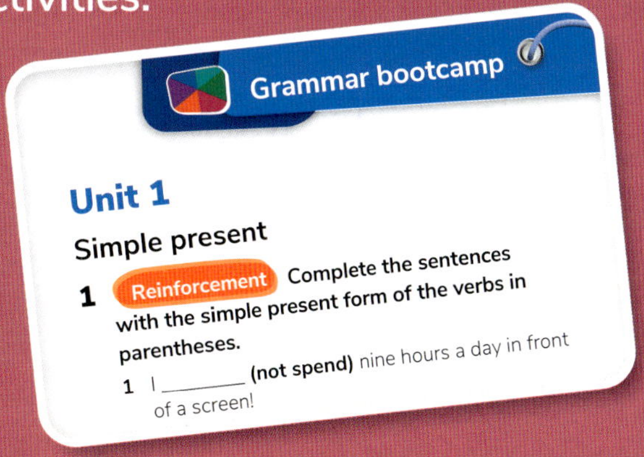

Grammar bootcamp

Unit 1

Simple present

1 Reinforcement **Complete the sentences with the simple present form of the verbs in parentheses.**

1 I ________ **(not spend)** nine hours a day in front of a screen!

LISTENING	REAL-WORLD SPEAKING	WRITING	PRONUNCIATION	PROJECT
Grammar: possessive adjectives, likes and dislikes, *Wh-* questions, question words, *there is/are*, object pronouns				
A live report from a public library **Subskill:** Answering true/false questions	Expressing preferences	A review **Subskill:** *also, too* and *as well*	/s/ /z/ /ɪz/	Make a storyboard for a movie or a book. **Creativity** Generating ideas together
A podcast about First Nations people of Canada **Subskill:** Identifying key words in questions	Asking for clarification	An email to an e-pal **Subskill:** *because* and *because of*	/ʊ/ and /u/	Create a fold-out poster about life 25 years ago where you live. **Communication** Taking turns
A presentation about the Afghan girls' robotics team **Subskill:** Writing notes	Telling a story	A story **Subskill:** Time expressions	Word linking	Make an infographic about a success story. **Collaboration** Taking on different roles
An interview with the founder of a skills-sharing service **Subskill:** Choosing between options	Giving advice	Notes and messages **Subskill:** *too* + adjective, *not* + adjective + *enough*	Weak forms in comparatives	Make a proposal to get money for a business idea. **Communication** Communicating effectively in a formal situation to a group
A podcast about environment campaigners **Subskill:** Answering true, false and no information questions	Making decisions	An advertisement **Subskill:** Giving examples	Diphthongs /eɪ/ /aɪ/ /oʊ/	Conduct a green audit of your school and make proposals for change. **Critical thinking** Solving different types of problems
A conversation about finding a present **Subskill:** Noticing differences between the question and what you hear	Talking about experience	An e-postcard **Subskill:** *who, where* and *which*	Consonant clusters	Make memes of things for classmates to do before they're 18. **Collaboration** Working together to achieve your goals
An interview with a teenage minimalist **Subskill:** Justifying answers	Asking about lost and found objects	A personal email **Subskill:** Adjective order	*for, since* and sentence stress	Prepare a 'Me Box' and make a video of yourself talking about the items in it. **Creativity** Taking the initiative
A presentation given by a teacher at an Open Day **Subskill:** Recognizing feelings	Making offers and requests	A for-and-against essay **Subskill:** Balancing arguments	*have to*	Make a proposal for the final class at the end of the school year. **Critical thinking** Thinking about other people's interests
Listening: review of subskills		**Speaking:** review of Key phrases		**Writing:** review of subskills

Project planner p130 Irregular verbs p134

STARTER What do you know?

Meet two students

Vocabulary: introducing yourself, your likes and dislikes

1 **Read the profiles of two 8th grade students from New York, USA, and answer the questions.**

1 Where does Lucía's father live?
2 Who is Lucía's favorite actor?
3 Who is Juan?
4 Does Harley play football?
5 What type of food does Harley like?

2 **Read the profiles again and answer the questions. There may be more than one answer. Who ... ?**

1 lives with three other people
2 studies a language that they speak at home
3 doesn't speak other languages
4 follows a star on social media
5 talks about meeting friends at their favorite place

3 **Which person would you most like to meet? Tell your partner why.**

I'd like to meet Harley because I really like going to the gym. What about you?

I'd like to meet Lucía because I also like watching series on TV.

Name: Lucía **Age:** 13
Born in: Villa Nueva, Guatemala

I've got one brother, Juan. He's 10. We live with our mother and grandmother in New York. My father lives in Guatemala.

I speak Spanish with my family, English and a little French.

I like studying math, but my favorite subject is Spanish – it's so easy!

I like watching movies and TV series. My favorite actor is Finn Wolfhard. I love his Twitter® posts.

My favorite place is the park. I go there to meet my friends.

Name: Harley **Age:** 14
Born in: New York, USA

I've got two sisters and we live with my dad. He works in a store.

I just speak English. I can't speak any other languages.

My favorite subjects are history and P.E.

I like swimming and going to the gym. I also like watching football – I'm a big New York Giants fan. And I really like pasta!

My favorite places are the sports center and Gino's Italian restaurant.

4 Complete the table with words and expressions from the profiles.

School subjects	*math*
Sports	
Other free-time activities	
Places in a town	

5 Read the description of a daily routine. Which student from exercise 1 is speaking?

I get up and take a shower at about 7:00. I have breakfast and then I go to school. In the afternoon, I do my homework and I often go out and play sports. I have dinner with my sisters and go to bed at about 10:00, but I usually listen to music for another hour before I go to sleep.

6 Work in pairs. Write the phrases in the correct order for your day. Then find out if your partner does things in the same order.

brush my hair   brush my teeth
do homework   do free-time activities
finish school   get dressed   get up   go home
go to bed   go to school   go to sleep
have breakfast   have dinner   have lunch
make my bed   pack my bag   play sports
start school   take a shower   wake up

Grammar: possessive adjectives and *have got*

7 Match subject pronouns 1–7 with the correct possessive adjective in the box.

her   his   its   my   our   their   your

1 I   2 she   3 we
4 you   5 it   6 they
7 he

8 Complete the table.

Affirmative/negative			
I/you/we/ they	1 ______ haven't (have not)	got	a sister. a brother. cousins. pets.
2 ______ 3 ______ 4 ______	's (has) 5 ______		

9 Complete the text with possessive adjectives and the correct form of *have got*.

Name: Shawna
Age: 14
Born in: Boston

I live with **1** ________ mom and **2** ________ husband, Ricky. I **3** ________ a sister named Meadow. I **4** ________ any brothers.

I speak English and a little French.

My classmates and I really like **5** ________ new music teacher. **6** ________ name is Mr. Dawson. Our school **7** ________ a good orchestra.

I'm a big fan of Rihanna and Lorde. I love **8** ________ music.

My favorite place is the shopping center. I love **9** ________ stores and it **10** ________ some nice cafés.

Grammar: likes and dislikes

10 Read the examples and write sentences.

I like watching TV.   She doesn't like swimming.
We hate getting up early.
They love photography.   He likes pasta.

love(s)	like(s)	don't/ doesn't like	hate(s)
😍	🙂	😣	😡

1 I / 😡 / get up / early.
2 She / 😍 / watch videos on YouTube™.
3 We / 🙂 / our math teacher.
4 They / 🙂 / live in the center of the city.
5 He / 😣 / pizza.

11 Write two things you love, two things you like, two things you don't like and two things you hate. But write them in any order!
Star Wars™, playing the piano, cleaning my room ...

12 Work in pairs. Look at your partner's notes and try to guess which things they love, like, don't like and hate.

Reinforcement and Challenge   Grammar bootcamp p116

Let's get personal!

Vocabulary: personal information

1 **Complete the profile with the missing headings in the box.**

Family   Favorite things   Hobbies   School   The facts

1 ________
Age: 14
Birthday: November 19th
Hometown: Berlin
Languages: German, English

2 ________
Sister: Ada, 11 years old
Brother: Denis, 8 years old

TANER

3 ________
8th grade
Mr. Fischer
Favorite subject: art

4 ________
Food: chicken and vegetables
Music: hip hop and rap
Singer/actor: Tom Holland
Color: black

5 ________
Listening to music
Hanging out with friends

2 1 **Listen to Taner's friend asking about the profile. Correct the incorrect information.**
Taner's birthday is on November 17th.

3 **Listen again and add any missing information.**

Grammar: *Wh-* questions

4 **Complete the personal information questions.**

1 Where ________________ from?
2 How old ________________ ?
3 When ________________ birthday?
4 What languages ________________ speak?
5 ________________ any brothers or sisters?
6 How ________________ spell that?

5 **Order the words to make questions.**

1 what's / favorite / your / subject ?
2 favorite / your / what's / food ?
3 who's / actor or singer / favorite / your ?
4 your / favorite / what's / color ?
5 of / music / you / what / do / kind / like ?
6 you / do / what / do / in / free time / your ?

6 **Work in pairs. What do you know about your partner? Make notes individually.**
Name: ________________________________
____
____

7 **Ask your partner the questions in exercises 4 and 5 to check if the information is correct. Add any missing information.**

Where are you from?

I live in Mexico City now, but I'm from a town outside the city.

Great. And what languages can you speak?

I can speak Spanish, French and some English.

8 **Make a profile of your partner like the one in exercise 1.**

Reinforcement and Challenge   Grammar bootcamp p116

A world of languages

Vocabulary: countries and languages

1 Complete the table with the languages of the countries.

Country	Language
China	1 *Chinese*
France	2
Italy	3
Japan	4
Mexico	5
Portugal	6
Turkey	7

Language note

Remember that countries, nationalities and languages start with a capital letter.

2 Work in pairs. Which language do you think these English words come from? Match them with a language in exercise 1.

1 alligator ________
2 banana ________
3 café ________
4 karate ________
5 ketchup ________
6 kiosk ________
7 umbrella ________

3 2 Listen and check your answers.

Grammar: question words

4 Match the question words in the box with the information we use them for.

How How many What Where Which Who ~~Why~~

1 a reason *Why*
2 a person ________
3 a number ________
4 an object ________
5 a place ________
6 to give options ________
7 the way to do something ________

5 Complete the quiz with question words.

What do you know about languages?
Take the Language quiz.

1 *How many* languages are there in the world?
a 7,000 **b** 500 **c** 3,500

2 ________ is the most common language?
a English **b** Spanish **c** Chinese

3 ________ invented the 'Elvish' languages in literature?
a William Shakespeare (*Romeo and Juliet*)
b J. R. R. Tolkien (*Lord of the Rings*)
c J. K. Rowling (*Harry Potter*)

4 ________ of these places has 500 words for 'rain'?
a Hawaii, USA **b** Mawsynram, India
c Tutendo, Colombia

5 La Gomera, an island in Spain, has a special language. ________ do people communicate?
a with smoke **b** with pigeons
c by whistling

6 ________ can you hear 'Chalcatongo Mixtec'?
a in Mexico **b** in Brazil
c in Papua New Guinea

7 ________ is International Language Day?
a January 1st **b** February 21st **c** June 3rd

6 Work in pairs. Answer the quiz questions.

7 3 Listen to the radio show. Check your answers to the quiz.

FUN FACTS

There are more than 200 invented languages in books and movies. Klingon is an invented language in the television series *Star Trek*™. You can read Shakespeare's *Hamlet* in Klingon!

Grammar: *there is/are*

1 **Read the examples. Complete the table with the words in blue.**

How many languages are there in the world?
There's a special language in La Gomera.
There aren't 500 words for rain.
Is there an invented language in *Romeo and Juliet*?
No, there isn't.

Affirmative/Negative		
1 ________ / There isn't	a special language.	
There are / 2 ________	500 words for rain.	
Questions		**Short answers**
3 ________	a special language?	Yes, there is. No, 4 ________ .
Are there	500 words?	Yes, there are. No, there aren't.
How many languages	5 ________ ?	

2 **Complete the questions and answers with the correct form of *there is/are*.**

FUN FACTS about languages

1 Q: ________ an official language in the USA?
A: No, ________ an official language in the USA, but most people think it's English.

2 Q: How many words for color ________ in Pirahã, a language in Brazil?
A: None. ________ any words for color in Pirahã.

3 Q: ________ any languages with one speaker?
A: Yes. ________ a language called Yaghan in Argentina with only one speaker.

4 Q: How many letters ________ in the Cambodian alphabet?
A: ________ 74 letters/characters.

5 Q: How many words ________ in English?
A: ________ over 250,000.

Grammar: object pronouns

3 **Read the examples, then match subject pronouns 1–7 with object pronouns a–g.**

La Gomera has a special language. Some students learn it in school.
They whistle. You can hear them.

1 I	a him
2 you	b us
3 he	c them
4 she	d me
5 it	e it
6 we	f you
7 they	g her

4 **Complete the sentences with an object pronoun.**

1 This is Ellen's dictionary. Can you give it to ________ ?
2 I love video games. I play ________ every weekend.
3 Our teacher gives ________ homework after every class.
4 I don't understand this exercise. Can you help ________ ?
5 What do you think of Justin Bieber? I love ________ !

5 **Work in pairs. Ask each other questions about the people or things in the box.**

comic books Daisy Ridley homework
horror movies ice cream Neymar
Selena Gomez shopping video games

6 **Circle the correct option.**

Melissa May, a British teenager, loves **1 learn/learning** languages. She can **2 to speak/speak** German, French and Spanish, and she **3 read/reads** in five more languages. She also **4 is speaking/speaks** 'Sknvnns' – a language that she invented.

The language **5 have got/has got** 1,500 words, and **6 there is/there are** two ways to write **7 their/them** – using the normal alphabet and using symbols.

Melissa May lives with **8 his/her** father, but she **9 can't/don't** speak the language to **10 he/him**. She's the only person who speaks **11 it/him**!

What's in this book?

1 **Look through the book and answer the questions.**

1 Where is the Quick review in each unit?
2 What can you do on pp116–127?
3 Where can you look for the past form of an irregular verb?
4 What information is on p128?

2 **There are lots of things to help you in the book. Find the answers to the questions.**

1 What's the **WDYT?** question in Unit 4?
2 What's question 2 in **Video skills** in Unit 7?
3 What's the **Reading subskill** in Unit 6?
4 What's the last word you study in **Word work** in Unit 8?
5 Who's the **Celebrity corner** in Unit 5?
6 What's question 3 in the **Critical thinking** activity in Unit 3?
7 What's the **Listening subskill** about in Unit 1?
8 What **Super skill** do you practice in the Project in Unit 2?

3 **Add the phrases in bold in exercise 2 to the sentences.**

1 In the *Reading subskills* you learn how to be a more effective reader.
2 In the ________________ sections, you learn to think critically about videos.
3 In the ________________ activities, you learn to think more carefully about ideas in a text.
4 In the ________________ sections, you practice abilities which are important in everyday life.
5 In the ________________ activities, you meet new vocabulary in context in our reading texts.
6 In the ________________ questions, you think about a big question at the start of the unit.
7 In the ________________ , you learn how to be a more effective listener.
8 In the ________________ you learn about a famous person and how they're related to the topic.

4 **Who or what are these? In which unit do you meet them?**

1 ________________

2 ________________

3 ________________

4 ________________

5 ________________

6 ________________

7 ________________

8 ________________

9 ________________

10 ________________

5 **Work in pairs. Complete the challenge.**

Classroom Challenge

1 In which unit do you learn about the chores that girls do at home?
2 In which unit do you talk about your favorite video games?
3 In which unit do you make a video about your Me Box?
4 Where do you 'Think – Plan – Create – Present'?
5 In which unit do you do a hieroglyphics puzzle?
6 In which unit do you find out about Renata Flores?
7 In which unit do you study zero and first conditional?
8 In which unit do you talk about money?
9 In which project do you make a storyboard?
10 In which unit do you identify a bank robber?

1 Stories

WDYT?
(What do you think?)

What makes a good story?

Video skills p13

Real-world speaking p19

Project pp22–23

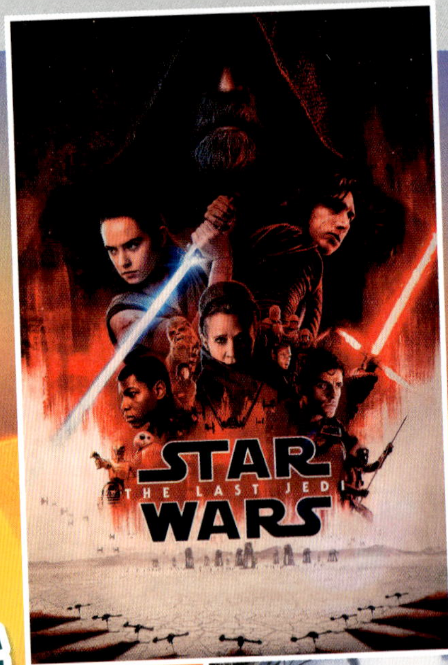

My top 5 movies

1. *Star Wars*: this classic **science-fiction movie** is fantastic!
2. *P.S. I Still Love You*: Sunday afternoon? Couch? If it's the time to watch a **romantic movies,** this is for you.
3. *Maze Runner*: I love a good **thriller** and the movies in this series are great.
4. *Superman*: this is my favorite **superhero movie**.
5. *Monster House*: I'm not a big fan of **horror movies,** but my little sister thinks *Monster House* is cool.

My top 5-4-3...

TV, movies and games

1 Complete the Screen time questionnaire.

2 Work in pairs. Compare your answers to the questionnaire.

What about question 1?

I look at all of them except a movie theater screen.

I don't have a tablet, but I look at all the others, except the movie theater of course! How about question 3? Who plays video games in your family?

My brother, he plays *Age of Empires*® all day, but I think it's really boring.

Screen time

1. **Which screens do you look at in a typical day?**
   - computer
   - cell phone
   - tablet
   - TV
2. **How many hours a day do you spend looking at a screen on a weekday?**
   And on the weekend?
3. **In your family, who ... ?**
   - watches TV shows
   - follows YouTubers
   - goes to the movies
   - watches a TV series on a platform like Netflix®
   - plays video games
   - watches movies at home
   - uses social media

My top 4 TV shows

1 *The Voice*: I love singing, so I always watch this **talent show**.

2 *Stranger Things*: This **drama series** about Eleven and her friends is really cool.

3 *Adventure Time*: I'm into **cartoons**, so the adventures of Finn and Jake are perfect for me!

4 *Junior MasterChef*: I love cooking and this competitive **cooking show** is my favorite show.

My top 3 games

1 *Age of Empires*: In this historical **strategy game**, you're the leader: can you make the right decisions?

2 *Legend of Zelda*: Try to save Princess Zelda in this great fantasy **action game**.

3 *Monster Hunter Stories*: I love **role-playing games** and for me, this is the best!

Remembering new vocabulary

To help you remember new vocabulary, think of an example that is important to you. For example, *Minecraft*® is my favorite **construction game**.

3 **Write an example for each type of movie, show or game in the box.**

a comedy show · a construction game · a documentary · a music show · a musical · a sports game · a sports show · a travel show · an action movie

an action movie: Godzilla vs. Kong

4 **Work in pairs. Student A says an example. Student B says the type of movie, show or game.**

OK – *Minecraft*?

It's a construction game.

5 **Read the information from the website and match the words in bold with the definitions.**

1 a movie or TV show using animation ________
2 a TV show about cooking ________
3 a movie about love ________
4 a game in which players pretend to be imaginary characters ________
5 a movie which makes you feel afraid ________
6 a movie in a future world ________
7 a book or movie with an exciting story ________
8 a fast-moving and exciting game ________
9 a television competition for singers, musicians, etc ________
10 a game in which you think carefully and make decisions ________
11 a TV show which tells a story in parts ________
12 a movie about a person with special powers ________

6 **Write your own Top 5, 4, 3 ... and be ready to explain why you like each thing.**

7 **Work in pairs. Compare your list with a partner. Do you like the same things?**

VIDEO SKILLS

8 **This video is called 'A visit to the film studio'. What actions do you think you are going to see? Watch and check.**

9 **Work in pairs. Discuss the questions.**

1 Who made this video?
2 What type of person would like this video?
3 What is the main reason for the video?
   a to give facts about making films, or movies
   b to entertain
   c to give information about a film, or movie

A blog post

1 4 **Listen to the extracts from movies and TV shows. What type are they?**

2 **Work in pairs. Discuss the questions for each of the three photos.**

1 What are the people doing in the photo?
2 What do you think they are making?

a cartoon   a documentary   a movie
a music video   a talent show
a travel show   a video game

Subskill: Making and checking predictions

Before you read, note words connected to the topic of the text. Look for these words in the text to help you decide if your predictions were correct.

3 5 **Note words connected with the activities in exercise 2. Read and listen to the text and check if your predictions were correct.**

4 **Read the text again. Who ... ?**

1 started being creative at a young age
2 has the opportunity to meet people locally and share ideas
3 probably makes videos once a week
4 meets important people because of their work
5 works on their project every day
6 works with a group of people

5 **Read the text again. Match 1–8 to a–h to make sentences about the text.**

1 Zachary uses his films
2 Today you don't need a camera
3 Lisa and Lena are very popular
4 David Eisman is
5 You can get help online
6 Lisa and Lena's videos
7 Ross recommends a program

a for people who want to make cartoons.
b to make films.
c are better than Zoey's.
d to show problems in his area.
e on social media.
f a good organizer.
g or from your arts center.

6 Word work **Match the definitions to the words in bold in the text.**

1 people who regularly read someone's social media ________
2 a small machine for playing video games ________
3 send data from your computer to a larger computer system or to the internet ________
4 nervous about speaking to people ________
5 a part of a town ________
6 two children who were born at the same time to the same mother ________

7 **The words in bold are in the wrong sentence. Correct the sentences.**

1 My brother and I are **followers**, but we look very different ________
2 I often feel very **upload** when I meet new people. ________
3 I have a **neighborhood**, but I don't spend much time playing video games. ________
4 I have 30 **twins** on Instagram®. ________
5 Our **console** is changing fast: there are lots of new cafés and stores now. ________
6 Can you help me **shy** these photos? ________

CRITICAL THINKING — SUPER SKILLS

1 **Remember** Which different types of technology were in the reading text?
2 **Evaluate** Which of the people in the text do you think are making ... ?
   a the best use of technology
   b the most creative use of technology
3 **Create** How would you like to be creative with technology?

TechMaster

Screen time? Screen-tastic!

Some adults say that teens are always in front of a computer screen or playing games on a **console**. But what about the positive side to technology? In today's TechMaster post we meet four people who use modern tech to get super creative.

Zachary Maxwell is a teenager from New York. He describes himself as **shy**, but he has meetings with politicians. Why do they meet him? Because of his videos. Zachary made his first documentary when he was eight. He often uses his films to raise awareness about problems in his school or **neighborhood**. Zach uses a camera to make his films, but don't worry if you don't have one; with a phone, anyone can become a film-maker today.

The app Musical.ly (now called TikTok®) helped 16-year-old **twins**, Lisa and Lena Mantler from Germany, to become social media superstars. The sisters spend 20 minutes a day making videos to post on the app and now have over 16 million **followers**.

When he was 16, David Eisman started Pixelman Productions. David doesn't write programs. He organizes the team. They're working on their first game, *Mirka*. If you're into video games, why not make one yourself? At make-video-games.com there are lots of tutorials and programs to help you make an awesome strategy game.

COMMENTS

Zoey: I normally **upload** a video on TikTok once a week. But I'm not as good as Lisa and Lena!

Reply

TechMaster: No problem Zoey – the important thing is having fun!

Ross: I use an app called Animaker™ to make cartoons.

Reply

TechMaster: Great Ross – thanks for sharing!

Candy K: My local arts center has a film-making club three times a month.

Reply

TechMaster: Yes – arts centers can be good places to get help and ideas.

Simple present

1 Read the examples and the Spelling rules on p21 to complete the rules.

He **uses** an app called *Animaker*.
David **doesn't do** programming.
Why **do** politicians **meet** him?
Do they **post** videos on social media?
Yes, they **do**.

1 After *he/she/it*, the verb ends in __ / __ / __ .
2 To make the negative, use __ / __ + base form.
3 To make the question, use __ / __ + base form.
4 Answer *Yes/No* questions with *yes* + subject + __ / __ , or *no* + subject + __ / __ .

2 Rewrite the sentences in the affirmative, negative or question form.

1 I don't like documentaries. (+)
I like documentaries.
2 My grandmother likes watching talent shows. (–)
3 Her brother doesn't use a game console. (?)
4 We don't play construction games. (+)
5 Their teacher shows videos in class. (?)

Adverbs and expressions of frequency

3 Look at the examples. Which one gives a specific idea of frequency and which two describe frequency in general?

He **often** uses films to talk about problems.
I upload a video on TikTok **once a week**.
Teens are **always** in front of a screen.

Frequency expressions
once = one time   twice = two times

4 Divide the expressions in the box into two groups: 'specific frequency' and 'general frequency'.

always five times a week four times a day hardly ever never often once a month once a week sometimes three times a month twice a day twice a year usually

5 Write the expressions in each group in order from most frequent to least frequent.

Specific: *four times a day, ...*
General: *always, ...*

6 Look at the examples in exercise 3 and circle the correct option to complete the rules.

1 With the verb *be*, general adverbs come **before/after** the verb.
2 With other verbs, general adverbs come **before/after** the verb.
3 With specific frequency, the expression comes at the **beginning/end** of the sentence.

7 Order the words to make sentences.

1 plays video games / my father / never
2 once a week / we / our art class / have
3 on social media / we / upload videos / sometimes
4 I / twice a year / a new video game / get
5 hardly ever / I / with my phone / film things

8 Insert the adverbs and expressions of frequency in the correct position in the text.

How often do you use screens?

1 I use screens for five hours a day **(sometimes)**. **2** We use computers in school and I play video games with my friends after school **(three times a week; usually)**. **3** I go to the movies and I read books **(about four times a year; hardly ever)**. **4** My school celebrates Screen-Free Week **(once a year)**. **5** We all sign a Screen-Free promise card and they organize special activities like sports and competitions **(usually)**. It's really fun, but I'm happy it's only one week a year!

9 Answer the question to solve the Brain teaser.

B R A I N TEASER

1 What can you always find in the middle of March?
2 Which English word do people always pronounce badly?
3 What goes up once a year and never comes down?

What are the answers to these riddles?

Phrases with prepositions: likes and dislikes

1 Read the flyer. Which activity would you like to do?

CITY LIBRARY

Welcome to the City Library.
It's more than a place to read books!

- Create a comic book with the latest computer programs.
- Make a video about a book.
- Record a review for our podcast.
- Join a writing workshop.

Read what teens say about our activities:

'I'm **not very fond of** reading, but I'm **really into** the activities here.'

'I'm a **big fan of** fantasy novels. I'm making a podcast about *Eragon*®.'

'I'm **not crazy about** technology, but I love drawing my own graphic novels.'

'I'm **really good at** telling stories, but I'm **interested in** trying new things.'

2 Use the flyer to complete the phrases.

1 I'm (not) very fond ________ reading.
2 I'm (not) really ________ the activities here.
3 I'm (not) a big fan ________ fantasy novels.
4 I'm (not) crazy ________ technology.
5 I'm (not) good ________ telling stories.
6 I'm (not) really interested ________ trying new things.

3 Look at the phrases in exercise 2 and answer the questions.

1 Which five phrases mean *I like*/*I don't like*?
2 Which phrase means *I can*/*can't ... well*?
3 Apart from nouns, what else do we use after prepositions?

4 Work in pairs. Talk about the topics in the box using the phrases in exercise 2.

comic books cooking football painting social media snowboarding video games

I'm not really into comic books.

Really? I'm a big fan of *Teen Titans*.

A live report

5 6 A reporter is talking to students at the library. Which activities from the flyer in exercise 1 are they doing?

1 Annabelle ________________________________

2 Noah and Josh ________________________________

Subskill: Answering true/false questions

Before you listen, read each sentence carefully and underline key words. All the information in a sentence must be correct for it to be true.

6 Listen again. Are the sentences true or false? Give reasons for your answers.

1 Annabelle talks about books in her videos.
2 Her videos help people to choose which books to read.
3 She's crazy about horror stories.
4 Noah and Josh are using technology in their workshop.
5 They are using photos and maps to practice writing.
6 The activities they do will help them with their future jobs.
7 They aren't interested in science fiction.

7 Work in pairs. What are some ways to encourage people your age to read more?

CELEBRITY CORNER

Reese Witherspoon has a book club where she recommends books to her fans. Find two more celebrities who have a book club.

Simple present and present progressive

1 Read the examples. Are the verbs in the simple present or present progressive?

Today, I**'m visiting** the City Library.
I **come** here twice a week.
How often **do** you **come** here?
What **are** you **doing** here?
You **aren't reading**.
She **doesn't like** horror stories.

2 Complete the rules with *SP* (simple present) or *PP* (present progressive).

1 We use the ________ to talk about actions that are in progress now, or around now.
2 We use the ________ to talk about routines or habits.
3 We often use the ________ with *always, sometimes, never, every day, once a week, twice a month*, etc.
4 We often use the ________ with *now, today, right now*.

3 Write the verbs in the simple present or present progressive.

1 I ________ **(read)** a romantic novel right now.
2 My friends and I usually ________ **(play)** video games on the weekend.
3 I ________ **(not like)** writing, but my brother often ________ **(write)** for our school magazine.
4 Now, everyone ________ **(watch)** the new season of *Sherlock* on Netflix.
5 Our school ________ **(not use)** digital books.
6 We ________ **(make)** a video review in class this week.

Remember!
We don't use the present progressive with some verbs, e.g. *be, like, love, want*.

4 Write questions in the simple present or present progressive. Then match the questions with the answers in exercise 3.

1 when / you / play video games ? __
2 how often / you / write / stories ? __
3 your school / use / digital books ? __
4 what TV series / everyone / watch / now ? __
5 you / read / anything / right now ? __
6 what / you / do / in class / this week ? __

5 Work in pairs. Ask and answer the questions in exercise 4.

6 Work in pairs. Student A chooses a verb. Student B asks questions to guess the verb.

cook eat read sit sleep swim work

Are you doing it right now?
No, I'm not.
Do you do it in your free time?
Yes, I do.
Is it swimming?
Yes, it is.

7 Circle the correct option.

GRAMMAR ROUND-UP
1 2 3 4 5 6 7 8

The Donkey Library

It's early on Saturday morning in La Gloria, a small town in Colombia. Most people are asleep, but not Luis Soriano. He **1 takes/is taking** books on his donkeys to villages that don't have a library.

Luis goes to the villages **2 every/twice** a week. As well as taking books, he also **3 help/helps** children with their homework. Luis **4 travels sometimes/sometimes travels** for four hours, but he **5 don't/doesn't** mind. The children **6 are always/always are** happy to see him. Why **7 he does/does he do** it? Well, Luis thinks that reading is important. He has over 4,000 books now, so he **8 builds/is building** a library near his home. But he will continue to take his donkey library to the villages.

Reinforcement and Challenge Grammar bootcamp p118

Expressing preferences

1 Look at the Sofastream screen. What would you choose to watch? Give reasons for your answer.

2 Watch the video. What do Hannah and Ross decide to watch?

3 Watch again. Which Key phrases do you hear?

4 Complete the dialogue with the Key phrases. Watch again and check.

Hannah Do you fancy watching something?

Ross Sure. What do you **1** ________ watch?

Hannah How about a TV series?

Ross That's what we always watch. I'd **2** ________ to watch a film.

Hannah How about *Mamma Mia! Here we go again*? You love the first film.

Ross I'm not really in the mood for a romantic film. I'd **3** ________ watch an action film.

Hannah OK, what about *Avengers: Endgame?* It's about a group of friends who try to save the world.

Ross Yes, but that's a superhero movie, and I'm not really into superheroes.

Hannah OK, **4** ________ rather watch *Men in Black International*? It's an action film and it's funny.

Ross Yes, **5** ________ better than *Avengers: Endgame*. Let's watch that.

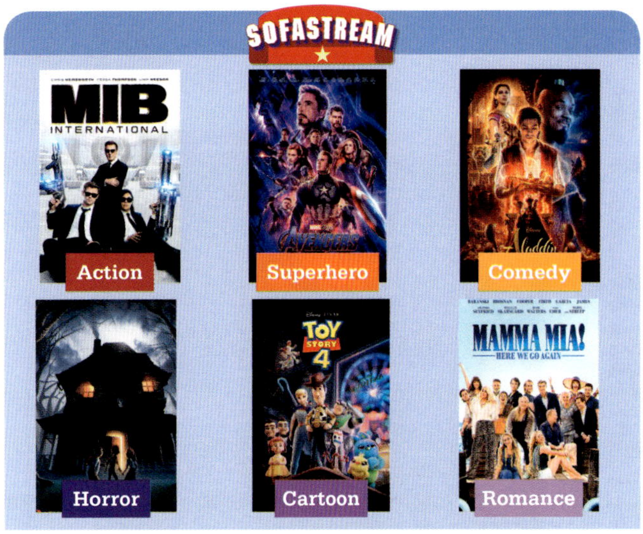

5 Create your own dialogue. Follow the steps in the Skills boost.

SKILLS BOOST

THINK

1 Choose a TV series or movie that you both want to watch. Think of reasons why.

2 Think of reasons why you **don't** want to watch three shows.

PREPARE

Prepare your dialogue. Make sure you use some Key phrases to ask and talk about preferences.

PRACTICE

Practice your dialogue. Take turns acting each part.

PERFORM

Act out your dialogue for the class.

6 Peer review **Listen to your classmates. Answer the questions.**

1 What do they decide to watch?

2 Which Key phrases did they use?

Key phrases

Asking about preferences: What do you want / would you like (to watch)?
Would you rather (watch) ... ?
Would you prefer (to watch) ... ?

Talking about preferences: I'd rather (watch) ...
I'd prefer (to watch) ...
I don't mind.
Maybe ... is a better idea.
It sounds better / more interesting / more fun than ...

UK → US

Do you fancy watching something? (UK) → Do you want to watch something? (US)

film (UK) → movie (US)

Book review

Divergent ★★★★★

Veronica Roth

Divergent is the first novel in a trilogy by American author Veronica Roth. It's science fiction and it's an adventure story too. It tells the story of Beatrice (Tris) and how she tries to find her true identity.

The story takes place in Chicago, sometime in the future. The city has five parts, each with a different personality (honest, selfless, kind, brave and smart). Beatrice grows up in the 'selfless' part, but she doesn't feel that she belongs there. When she's 16, she chooses to go to live with 'the brave'. She does tests to show that she really is brave. She also meets a boy named Four, and together they discover a secret that could hurt her family.

I love this book because it has interesting characters, and because it's exciting. There's action, humor and there's romance as well. I think it's the perfect book for people who love adventure stories. I really recommend it!

Naomi (15)

A review

1 **Work in pairs. Can you use the words in the box to talk about a movie, a book or both?**

acting author chapter character director music page special effects story writing

2 **Read the book review. Which questions does it answer?**

1 What's the name of the book?
2 What type of book is it?
3 What's it about?
4 Why does the writer like the book?
5 Who's the writer's favorite character?
6 What kind of people would like the book?

3 **Answer the questions in exercise 2.**

4 **Match paragraphs 1–3 with the information they contain.**

a information about the story __
b the name of the book, the author and what it's about __
c the writer's opinion of the book __

Subskill: *also*, *too* and *as well*

We use also, too and as well when we add extra information.

5 **Read the sentences. Find one other sentence with *also*, *too* and *as well* in the review.**

1 It's exciting. It's **also** very funny.
2 My favorite character is Beatrice, but I like Four **too**.
3 It's a book, and it's a movie **as well**.

6 **Read the sentences in exercise 5 and complete the rules.**

1 ________ and ________ come at the end of sentence.
2 ________ usually comes after the verb *be* but before other verbs.

7 **Rewrite the sentences with *also*, *too* and *as well* in the correct position.**

1 I love romantic movies and I'm into **also** musicals.
2 The acting is great and I **too** love the music.
3 The story is good and **as well** there's action.
4 Tom Hanks is in the movie and **too** he's the director.
5 It's sad, but at times **also** it's funny.
6 I like the book and I **as well** like the movie.

8 **Write a review about a book or a movie for a website. Follow the steps in the Skills boost.**

SKILLS BOOST

THINK

Think about a book or movie that you like. Make notes about it. Include the following:

- name ______
- type of book/movie ______
- author/director ______
- story ______
- your opinion of the book/movie ______
- who would like it ______

PREPARE

Organize the information into three paragraphs. Make notes about what each will contain.

______

WRITE

Write your review.

CHECK

Read your review and answer the questions.

1 Do you include information about the book/movie and give your opinion? ☐

2 Do you organize the information into three paragraphs? ☐

3 Do you use the simple present correctly? ☐

4 Do you use *also*, *too* and *as well*? ☐

9 Peer review **Exchange your review with another student. Would you like to read the book or see the movie? Why/why not?**

Quick review

Grammar

Simple present

Affirmative and negative

We use the simple present to talk about routines or habits.

*I **make** movies on my phone. He **makes** documentaries.*

*I **don't like** watching TV. He **doesn't make** comic books.*

Spelling rules for *he/she/it*

For most verbs, add *-s*: *sing* → *she sings*

For verbs that end in *-s*, *-sh*, *-ss*, *-ch*, *-x* or *-o*, add *-es*:

go → *it goes*   *teach* → *she teaches*

For verbs that end in consonant + *y*, omit *y* and add *-ies*:

study → *he studies*

Some verbs are irregular: *have* → *has*

***Wh-*, *yes/no* questions and short answers**

*What **do** you **do** in your free time?*

***Do** you **like** making movies?*   *Yes, I **do**.*

***Does** your phone **have** this app?*   *No, it **doesn't**.*

Adverbs and expressions of frequency

Adverbs of frequency (*always*, *sometimes*, *never*, etc.) come after the verb *be* and before other verbs.

*I am **never** late. My sister **sometimes** plays soccer.*

Expressions of frequency (*every day/week*, *once/twice/three times a month*) come at the end of a sentence.

*We go to the supermarket **twice a week**.*

Present progressive

We use the present progressive to talk about actions that are in progress now, or around now.

We often use the present progressive with *now*, *today*, *right now*.

***I'm reading** a good book right now.*

*He **isn't listening** to music.*

***Are** you **playing** a game? Yes, I **am**. / No, I**'m not**.*

Spelling rules for *-ing*

For most verbs: add *-ing* *buy* → *buying*

Verbs that end in *-e*: omit *e* and add *-ing* *take* → *taking*

Some verbs that end in consonant + vowel + consonant: double consonant and add *-ing* *swim* → *swimming*

Vocabulary

7 TV, movies and games

action game, action movie, cartoon, comedy show, construction game, cooking show, documentary, drama series, horror movie, musical, music show, role-playing game, romantic movie, science-fiction movie, sports game, sports show, strategy game, superhero movie, talent show, thriller, travel show

8 Phrases with prepositions: likes and dislikes

I'm (not) a big fan of ... , I'm (not) good at ... , I'm (not) really interested in ... , I'm (not) crazy about ... , I'm (not) very fond of ... , I'm (not) really into ...

1 Project

WDYT?
(What do you think?)

What makes a good story?

TASK: Make a storyboard for a movie or a book.

Learning outcomes

1 I can create and present a storyboard for a movie or a book.

2 I can generate new ideas.

3 I can use appropriate language from the unit.

Graphic organizer → Project planner p130

1 Watch a video of students presenting their storyboard. What does each student do during the presentation?

STEP 1: THINK

2 **Look at the storyboard in the Model project and discuss the questions.**

If you know the story ...

- Does the storyboard cover the main events?
- Is anything important missing?

If you don't know the story, does the storyboard give you an idea about ... ?

- the main characters in the story
- the main events
- where the story happens

3 **Work in groups of three and answer the questions about the storyboard.**

1 How many pictures are there?
2 How can you identify the main character?
3 Are the sentences long or short?
4 What tense are the verbs in?
5 Apart from the pictures and the text, what else can you see?

STEP 2: PLAN

4 **In your group, choose a movie or book you all know.**

5 **Individually, make notes on the characters, the place and the main points of the story.**

6 **Work together and write the story in nine points, with a maximum of three short sentences per point.**

STEP 3: CREATE

7 **Work in groups. Read the tips in the Super skills box and practice saying the Key phrases with your group.**

CREATIVITY — **SUPER SKILLS**

Generating ideas together

Tips

Think individually. Then share your ideas.
Take your time. Discuss before you decide.
Use everyone's ideas to get the best result.

Key phrases

Let's each think of one thing to include in this picture.
What's the most important thing to include?
How can I draw ... ?
OK, don't draw, let's think first.
Wait a minute.
What about ... ?

8 **Read the *How to* ... tips on p130. Then work together to produce your storyboard. Use the tips and Key phrases in the Super skills box.**

Model project

ROBIN HOOD

1

King Richard leaves England to go to fight.

2

The King's bad brother Prince John and the evil Sheriff of Nottingham take control of the country.

3

Robin Hood lives in the forest with his Merry Men (his friends). He robs the rich and gives to the poor. Prince John and the Sheriff are angry because they can't catch Robin, …

4

… so they organize an archery competition. Robin is the best and they know he will win.

5

Robin comes to the competition and wins.

6

Prince John and the Sheriff catch Robin.

7

Robin's men come and free him.

8

King Richard comes back.

9

Robin and the King send the Prince and the Sheriff to prison.

STEP 4: PRESENT

9 **Work with another group. Take turns presenting your storyboard.**

10 Peer review **As you listen to your classmates, answer the questions.**

1. Is the storyboard attractive to look at?
2. Do they explain it clearly?
3. If you know the story, does the storyboard give a good summary? If you don't know the story, would you like to read the book/see the movie?

1 FINAL REFLECTION

1 The task

Was the storyboard well presented and attractive?

Did you explain it clearly?

2 Super skill

Did you work together to generate ideas? Give examples.

3 Language

Did you use language from the unit? Give examples.

2 Then and now

WDYT?
(What do you think?)

What can we learn from history?

Vocabulary: everyday objects; life events

Grammar: simple past; *could*; time expressions; *used to*

Reading: a history magazine about the Aztec world

Listening: a podcast about First Nations people of Canada

Speaking: asking for clarification

Writing: an email to an e-pal

Project: create a fold-out poster about life 25 years ago where you live

Video skills p25

Real-world speaking p31

Project pp34–35

HISTORY THROUGH OBJECTS

A 

B 

C 

D 

E 

F 

Everyday objects

1 **Match definitions 1–9 with the words in the box.**

board game bottle calculator musical instrument paper ruler socks sunglasses toothbrush

1 You use this to draw lines and check distances. ________________
2 A guitar and piano are types of this. ________________
3 People wear these on their feet, under their shoes. ________________
4 You wear these to protect your eyes from the sun. ________________
5 You carry water or other liquids in this. ________________
6 You use this to do math. ________________
7 Chess and Monopoly® are types of this. ________________
8 You use this to clean your teeth. ________________
9 You write on this with a pen or pencil. ________________

2 **Look at the ancient objects. What do you think people used them for?**

G

H

I

J

K

L

3 **Match 1–12 with ancient objects A–L.**

1  comb F

2  key __

3  scissors __

4  calendar __

5 

chewing gum __

6  knife and fork __

7  spoon __

8  dice __

9  alarm clock __

10  mirror __

11  change purse __

12  helmet __

4 **Complete the sentences about the ancient objects with the words in the box.**

alarm clock   chewing gum   comb
dice   key   knife   spoon

1 The Greek philosopher Plato invented the _________ because his students often arrived late for class.
2 People first used a _________ to eat soup. Later, they used a _________ to cut meat, and only later a fork.
3 In Roman times, only rich people carried a _________ because other people didn't need to lock their doors.
4 Thousands of years ago, people used a _________ to remove insects from their hair!
5 In ancient times, people didn't use _________ to play games, they used them to predict the future.
6 This piece of _________ is over 5,000 years old, but you can still see the tooth marks of a teenager in it!

5 **Write the names of objects from this page.**

1 things you find in the classroom
2 things you wear or carry
3 things you use to look good
4 things you use in your free time

6 **Work in pairs. Talk about the objects. Which do you often, sometimes or never use?**

How often do you use an alarm clock?

Never, I use my cell phone.

VIDEO SKILLS

7 **The video is called 'Living in 1927'. What do you think you will see? Watch and check.**

8 **Work in pairs. Discuss the questions.**

1 What did you learn from the video?
2 What is the message of the video?
3 Do you think this video is a good way to learn about history? Why/Why not?

A history magazine

1 Work in pairs. Take the quiz.

AMAZING AZTECS!

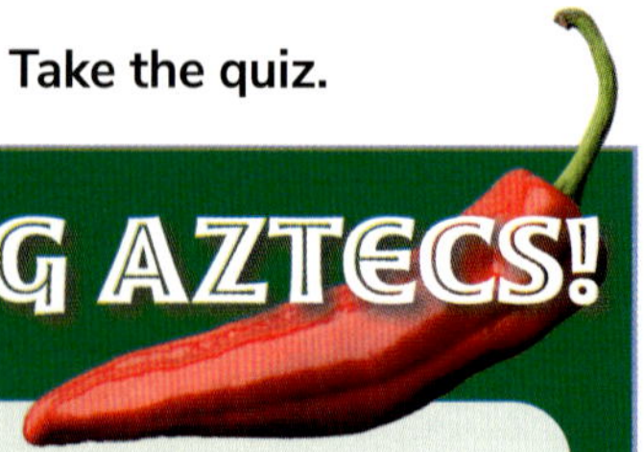

How much do you know about the Aztecs? Are the sentences true or false?

1 The Aztecs used cocoa beans to make a chocolate drink, and as dice when they played board games.
2 The Aztecs ate a lot of meat and fish. They also ate insects and frogs!
3 The Aztecs didn't have paper. Instead, they wrote on stone.
4 Many English words like *tomato, chocolate, avocado* and *chili* come from the Aztec language.
5 There was no popcorn or chewing gum in the time of the Aztecs.

2 9 Listen and check your answers.

▶ Subskill: Using visuals to understand ideas

You often find pictures and captions in articles. Look at the pictures and read the captions. They help you understand the text.

3 Read the text quickly. Look at the pictures and captions. Circle the ideas in the box that the text talks about.

building a city building roads calculating time education farming medicine

4 10 Read and listen to the text. Complete the sentences with words from the text.

1 The Aztecs decided to build their city in _________ .
2 They also built _________ to grow food and _________ to bring water to homes.
3 They had new ideas about education because _________ went to school.
4 They made a calendar _________ and a calendar _________ .
5 Today, people use their musical instruments, food and their _________ .

5 Answer the questions. Why did the Aztecs ... ?

1 create artificial islands
2 need to grow more food
3 make special gardens
4 build aqueducts
5 want all children to go to school
6 stay at home on certain days

6 Word work Match the definitions to the words in bold in the text.

1 the way that a person acts _________
2 clean, new _________
3 the effect on how people do things _________
4 not natural _________
5 with a special ability to do a job _________
6 put plants in the ground and look after them _________

7 Complete the sentences with words from exercise 6.

1 Chips and cereals often contain _________ ingredients.
2 Celebrities can have a big _________ on teenagers.
3 Can you open the window? I need some _________ air!
4 Teaching is an interesting and _________ job.
5 Our teacher wasn't happy with our _________ in class today.
6 We _________ oranges and apples in my country.

CRITICAL THINKING — SUPER SKILLS

1 **Understand** List the inventions and new ideas from the Aztec Empire.

2 **Evaluate** Which ideas do you think are most important? Think about:

- building new cities – now and in the future
- water in homes
- growing food
- education

3 **Create** What other inventions from the past are important now? Think of three and say why they're important.

CELEBRITY CORNER

Actor **Cole Sprouse** is a big fan of history. What did he study in college?

How the Aztecs changed the WORLD

The city in a lake

We live in a time of advanced technology, and we often think of ancient civilizations as 'primitive'. It's easy to forget that they invented many amazing things.

One of these civilizations was the Aztec Empire. When the early Aztecs arrived in the Valley of Mexico in around AD 1250, they decided to live on an island in Lake Texcoco. There wasn't much land, so they created **artificial** islands and built on these. With time, the capital city Tenochtitlan became larger than Rome. There were pyramids, stores and homes, all connected with canals and boats.

Farms on water

As there were more and more people in the city, the Aztecs needed more food. They couldn't **grow** vegetables in the water, so they created special 'floating' gardens on the water. And because the water in the lake wasn't good for drinking, they built aqueducts to bring **fresh** water to homes.

Boys and girls, both rich and poor, went to school in the Aztec Empire. The Aztecs knew that they needed **skilled** workers, so they were the first to start a system of free education. Everyone learned good **behavior**, but smart students could become engineers, scientists, artists or doctors.

New ideas about time

The Aztecs also created two calendars, one for festivals and the other for counting days. The second calendar had 365 days and 18 months, each with 20 days. There were five extra days that the Aztecs thought were unlucky, and on these days, they usually stayed at home!

More than a million people still speak Nahuatl, the Aztec language. People still play a type of drum invented by the Aztecs, and many Mexican recipes use ingredients from Aztec times. The Aztec Empire disappeared hundreds of years ago, but we can see its **influence** today.

(there) was/were

1 Read the examples and complete the rules.

The cocoa bean **was** important to the Aztecs.
Schools **weren't** only for rich children.
Was the water good for drinking? No, it **wasn't**.

The past of *be* is *I/he/she/it* **1** ________ and *you/we/they* **2** ________ .

To make the negative, add **3** ________ to the verb.

To make a question, change the order of the **4** ________ and the verb.

there was/were
There was no popcorn. (+ singular noun)
There were two calendars. (+ plural noun)

2 Complete the sentences with the simple past form of *be*.

Q: **1** ________ you interested in history when you **2** ________ younger?
A: No, I **3** ________ . I thought it **4** ________ boring!
Q: **5** ________ there a sports center in your town 20 years ago?
A: Yes, there **6** ________ , but there **7** ________ any skate parks.

could

3 Read the examples and circle the correct option.

Both boys and girls **could** go to school.
They **couldn't** grow vegetables on water.
Could they write on paper? Yes, they **could**.

1 We use *could* and *couldn't* to talk about **present/past** ability and possibility.
2 We **always/never** use *did* and *didn't* in negative sentences and questions.
3 After *could* and *couldn't*, we use the **infinitive/base form**.

4 Complete the sentences with *could* or *couldn't* and the ideas in the box.

become rich and famous   buy meat   do exercise   vote   watch chariot races

1 In Ancient Rome, there were gyms, so people ...
2 The politicians were all men, and women ...
3 There was a big stadium, where people ...
4 Fighting was important and gladiators ...
5 Most people were poor, so they ...

Past time expressions

5 Order the past time expressions from most recent to oldest.

a week ago   three years ago   in 2015   in June   in the 19th century   last night   when I was five   yesterday

6 Work in pairs. Ask questions using 'When was your last ... ' and the ideas in the box.

English class   exam   family celebration   meal in a restaurant   trip by bus   vacation

7 11 Complete the text with the correct past form of *be*, *could* or *couldn't*. Listen and check.

SCHOOL LIFE IN ANCIENT EGYPT

In some ways, schools in Ancient Egypt **1** ________ very similar to schools today. There **2** ________ tables and chairs in the classrooms, and there **3** ________ a type of paper called 'papyrus', so students **4** ________ write. They wrote using hieroglyphic symbols. There **5** ________ about 700 symbols in the Egyptian alphabet!

But most teenagers didn't go to school because education **6** ________ free. Only the sons of rich families **7** ________ study. Girls usually helped at home, and most of them **8** ________ read or write.

8 Answer the question to solve the Brain teaser.

TEASER

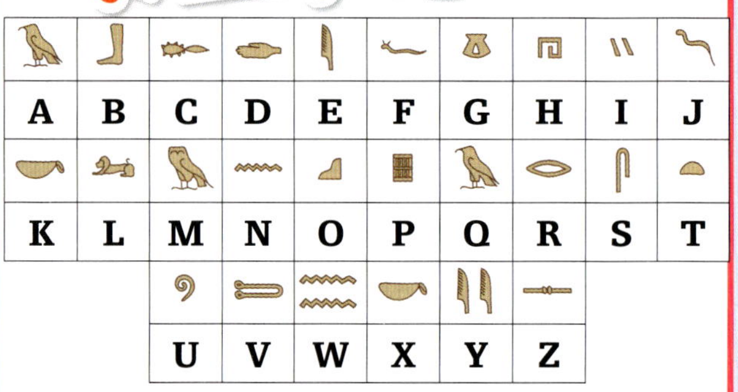

What is the word in Egyptian hieroglyphics?

Life events

1 **Look at the list of life events in the box and write them in a typical order.**

be born | die | get a job | get married | go to college | have children | leave high school | retire | start school | start work

2 **Match 1–3 with a–c. Which two things can you do at any time in your life?**

1 make friends __
2 grow up __
3 move __

a change from a child to an adult
b meet new people you like
c go to live in a different place

3 **The phrases in bold are in the wrong sentence. Correct the sentences.**

1 My mother was born in Colombia, but she **started school** when she was 20.
2 I'd like to study physics when I **retire.**
3 In Britain people **grow up** when they are 65.
4 I think it's better for children to **get a job** in the country than in the city.
5 I'd like to **leave high school** in television after I leave college.
6 I **moved to Spain** when I was four years old. I loved my first teacher.

A podcast

FUN FACTS

The First Nations is the name for more than 600 groups of indigenous people in Canada. There are over a million First Nations people in Canada today.

4 **Match captions 1–4 to photos A–D.**

1 __ Artist Michael Nicoll Yahgulanaas mixes traditional Haida art with manga.
2 __ The First Nations have their own snowboarding team.
3 __ Totem poles like this can be more than 12 meters tall. They represent family history and show important life events.
4 __ These pictures of life events are typical of the art of the Haida, one of the First Nations people from the northwest coast of Canada.

Subskill: Identifying key words in questions

Before you start, underline key words to help you recognize the questions when listening.

5 12 **Listen to a podcast about the First Nations in Canada. Number the questions in the order you hear them.**

a How many Haida are there today? __
b Where do First Nations people live today? __
c How many Haida were there? __
d What are the First Nations? *1*
e Is there a Haida language? __
f How did the Haida live in the past? __

6 **Listen again and answer the questions.**

1 Groups of indigenous people in Canada.

7 **Work in pairs. Discuss the questions.**

1 Do you or other people in different parts of your country speak more than one language?
2 Do you know if any traditional languages in your country are in danger?
3 How can we keep languages alive?

Simple past

1 Read the examples. Find two regular and two irregular verbs in the affirmative sentences. How do we form the negative?

Fifty people **lived** in one big longhouse.
Europeans **brought** new illnesses to the islands.
People **didn't speak** Haida.
In 2017 they **made** the first Haida movie.
People **married** someone from the other group.

2 Write the simple past of the verbs in the box. Look at the Irregular verbs list on pp134–135.

come do get go have like play read see start study talk think work write

3 Complete the sentences with the correct form of the verbs in parentheses.

1 The Maori ________ **(arrive +)** in New Zealand about 700 years ago.
2 They ________ **(go +)** 1,000 miles to New Zealand from Polynesia by boat.
3 They ________ **(have -)** maps: they ________ **(use +)** the sun and stars to navigate.
4 The Maori ________ **(call +)** the country Aotearoa, which means 'The Land of the Long White Cloud.'
5 Europeans ________ **(arrive -)** there until the 1600s.

4 Read the example and write *Wh*- questions about the underlined information in exercise 3.

How **did** the Haida **live?**

1 *When did the Maori arrive in New Zealand?*

used to

5 Read the examples and circle the correct option.

There **used to** be about 30,000 Haida.
People **didn't use to** live in individual houses.
Did people **use to** watch movies in Haida?

1 We use *used to* to talk about the **past/present/future**.
2 We use *used to* for **states and repeated actions/things we did once** in the past.
3 We only use *used to* in the **simple present/simple past**.
4 After *used to*, we write the verb in the **base form/-*ing* form**.

6 Complete the text about TV in the 1970s with the correct form of *used to*.

Most families in the 1970s only had one TV, so they all **1** ____________ **(watch +)** in the same room. Remote controls **2** ____________ **(exist -)**, so they couldn't change channels from their chair. People **3** ____________ **(have -)** computers, so you could only watch a series on TV and you **4** ____________ **(wait +)** a week for the next episode. Because there **5** ____________ **(be -)** many channels, everyone talked about the same shows.

7 Write questions about TV when you were six years old using *used to*.

1 how many hours / watch per day
2 where / watch TV
3 have / a favorite show
4 what channel / watch
5 watch TV / alone or with other people

8 Work in pairs. Ask your partner the questions in exercise 7.

9 Circle the correct option.

GRAMMAR ROUND-UP

1 2 3 4 5 6 7 8

Spencer O'Brien is a world champion snowboarder from Canada. Spencer is from the Haida Nation. First Nations people **1 didn't use to become/didn't used to become** top athletes, but now they **2 has/have** more opportunities to compete.

Spencer **3 could to/could** ski when she was only two, but she first tried snowboarding when she **4 were/was** 11. She **5 used to go/use to go** snowboarding for fun, but then she started to train more seriously. Later, Spencer represented Canada in the 2014 and 2018 Olympics® and she **6 wins/won** a gold medal at the 2016 X-Games®. When she **7 isn't competing/doesn't compete**, Spencer loves cooking. She **8 often works/works often** to help young First Nations people in sports too.

Reinforcement and Challenge Grammar bootcamp p119

Asking for clarification

1 Watch the video. What problems does Karen have on the phone?

2 Watch again. Which Key phrases do you hear?

3 Complete the dialogue with the Key phrases. Watch again and check.

Receptionist Good morning. How can I help?

Karen Oh, hello. I'd like some information about the Viking Museum please. Um, what **1** ________ it open?

Receptionist It's open from half past ten to half past three and from half past eleven at weekends.

Karen I'm **2** ________ ?

Receptionist 10:30 to 3:30 Monday to Friday and 11:30 to 3:30 at weekends.

Karen Ah, I see. And **3** ________ does it cost?

Receptionist Twelve fifty.

Karen Did you **4** ________ 'Twelve pounds fifty'?

Receptionist Yes, twelve pounds fifty.

Karen OK, and how can I **5** ________ ?

Receptionist Take the number 3 bus from the station.

Karen Could you **6** ________ ?

Receptionist Take the number 3 bus from the station to the museum.

Karen OK, thank you for your help. Goodbye.

4 Create your own dialogue. Follow the steps in the Skills boost.

SKILLS BOOST

THINK
Think of a place to visit and make notes or look up visitor information.

PREPARE
Prepare a dialogue. Remember to include Key phrases to ask for and clarify information.

PRACTICE
Practice your dialogue.

PERFORM
Act out your dialogue for the class.

5 **Peer review** Listen to your classmates. Answer the questions.

1 Which Key phrases did they use?
2 Would you like to visit this place?

Key phrases

Asking for information: What time does it open?
Is there a café?
How much does it cost?
How can I get there?

Checking information: Do you mean ... ?
Is that / Did you say ... ?

Asking someone to repeat: I'm sorry?
Sorry, I didn't get that.
Could you repeat that / say that again, please?

UK → US

at weekends (UK) → **on** weekends (US)
Monday **to** Friday (UK) → Monday **through** Friday (US)

Fraser To: Ekin Friday Attachments 1.4MB

1 Dear Ekin,

2 How are you? I hope your exams were OK. In your last letter, you asked me to tell you about my life when I was seven, so here you are!

3 We lived in a smaller house then and I used to share a room with my brother, Grant. We did more things together, but now he doesn't have much free time because of his job. Six years ago, we used to spend time playing soccer on our team or on our bikes. Now I do more things indoors and I like this house more because I have my own room.

4 Another difference is that I didn't use to go to school in the city. I went to the local school and I could have lunch at home because the school was very near our house. Sometimes in the winter our teacher couldn't get to school because of the snow, so we used to have the day off – it was great!

5 Now it's your turn: tell me about your life when you were seven!

6 Fraser

Me, when I was seven!

An email to an e-pal

1 Read the email from Fraser to his e-pal. Circle the best description a, b or c.

a what he likes about home and school

b how his life was different in the past

c how things are better now

2 Look at the email again. Match sections 1–6 with descriptions a–f.

a paragraph about school __

b opening paragraph to introduce the letter __

c signature of the writer __

d paragraph about home life __

e closing sentence asking the reader to write back __

f greeting the person he's writing to __

3 Read the email again. Are the sentences true, false or is there no information?

1 Fraser lives in a bigger house now.

2 Fraser is studying, so he spends less time with Grant now.

3 Fraser never plays soccer now.

4 He doesn't share a room now.

5 Fraser goes to school in his town.

6 He doesn't like his school lunch now.

Subskill: *because* and *because of*

When we give a reason, we use *because* and *because of*.

4 In the email, find two sentences with *because* and two sentences with *because of*.

5 Look at the sentences in exercise 4 and complete the rules.

1 ________ comes before a noun.

2 ________ comes before subject + verb.

6 Complete the sentences with *because* or *because of*.

1 I really enjoy history at school ________ the teacher.

2 That series was great ________ we could see how people lived a century ago.

3 I didn't enjoy the visit to the museum ________ the guide was very strict.

4 ________ the weather, we couldn't visit the Aztec pyramids.

7 **Write your reply to Fraser. Follow the steps in the Skills boost.**

SKILLS BOOST

THINK

1 Work in pairs. With your partner, write a list of things which were different when you were seven years old.

____

____

2 Choose two things and make notes about differences between the past and the present.

Subject	Past	Now
Home	*lived in a house*	*live in an apartment*

PREPARE

Organize your notes into sections. Use the same structure as Fraser's email.

____

____

____

____

____

____

____

____

____

WRITE

Individually, write your email. Use the example in exercise 1 to help you.

Dear Fraser,

How are you? ...

CHECK

Read your email and answer the questions.

1 Do you include interesting information about your life when you were seven? ☐

2 Do you explain reasons using *because* and *because of*? ☐

3 Do you use the simple past and *used to*? ☐

8 Peer review **Exchange your email with another student. Did you find out anything new about your classmate?**

Quick review

Grammar

(there) was/were

After *I/he/she/it* use *was/wasn't*.

Tenochtitlan ***was*** *a very big city.*

After *you/we/they* use *were/weren't*.

Some days in the Aztec calendar ***were*** *unlucky.*

Use *there was/wasn't* before a singular noun.

There wasn't *much land for growing food.*

Use *there were/weren't* before a plural noun.

There were *pyramids.*

could

Use *could/couldn't* + base form for ability in the past.

All Aztec children ***could*** *go to school.*

To make questions and negatives, don't use *do/don't*.

Could *the Aztecs drink the water in the lake? No, they* ***couldn't****.*

Past time expressions

These are some time expressions we use with the simple past:

yesterday, last night week/month/year, a week/month/year ago, in June/2015/the morning/the 20th century ...

Simple past

Some verbs are regular in the past: *loved, finished, tried*

Others are irregular: *be → was/were, do → did, see → saw*

To form questions and negatives, use *did*.

What time ***did*** *the movie* ***start****? 8 o'clock.*

Spelling rules

Most verbs: add *-ed*: *look**ed**, repeat**ed***

Verbs finishing with -e: add *-d*: *like**d**, create**d***

Verbs finishing consonant + *y*: change to *-ied*: *tr**ied**, repl**ied***

Verbs finishing consonant + vowel + consonant: double final consonant and add *-ed*: *pla**nned**, sto**pped***

used to

Use *used to* + base form to talk about states and repeated actions in the past.

I ***used to*** *go swimming. I* ***didn't use to*** *like vegetables.*

Did *you* ***use to*** *like One Direction?*

Vocabulary

🔊 13 Everyday objects

alarm clock, board game, bottle, calendar, calculator, change purse, chewing gum, comb, dice, helmet, key, knife and fork, mirror, musical instrument, paper, ruler, scissors, socks, spoon, sunglasses, toothbrush

🔊 14 Life events

be born, die, get a job, get married, go to college, grow up, have children, leave high school, make friends, move to a new house, retire, start school, start work

2 Project

WDYT?
(What do you think?)

What can we learn from history?

TASK: Create a fold-out poster about life 25 years ago where you live.

Learning outcomes

1 I can talk about my culture in the past.

2 I can communicate effectively, taking turns speaking and listening.

3 I can use appropriate language from the unit.

Graphic organizer → Project planner p130

1 Watch a video of students presenting their poster. What aspects of life do they talk about?

STEP 1: THINK

2 Look at the photos and read the Model project. What aspects of life can you see?

3 Where can you find information about life in the past where you live?

- the library
- the internet
- a book about ancient civilizations
- by talking to family

STEP 2: PLAN

4 In groups of four, look at the ideas in the box and choose two topics.

clothes and fashion communication entertainment family food the town

5 Think about what information each student is going to find and where.

6 Find the information.

STEP 3: CREATE

7 Work in groups. Read the tips in the Super skills box and practice saying the Key phrases with your group.

COMMUNICATION — SUPER SKILLS

Taking turns

Tips

Make sure each student speaks for the same amount of time.

Speak and then ask a question.

Listen and respond to what your partner says.

Key phrases

Can I stop you for a moment?

What do you think?

Can I say something?

Do you like that idea?

8 Share the information you have found and decide what to include. Use the tips and Key phrases in the Super skills box.

9 Create your poster.

Grammar and Vocabulary Quick review p33

Model project

1990s

Some free-time activities were the same in the past as they are now. A lot of people played sports and spent time with their families. But in the early 1990s, many people didn't have computers at home. They used to play video games and they watched TV in their free time, but there weren't many channels. Young people listened to music, but 25 years ago they listened to cassettes and CDs. A lot of people had a virtual pet called a Tamagochi®.

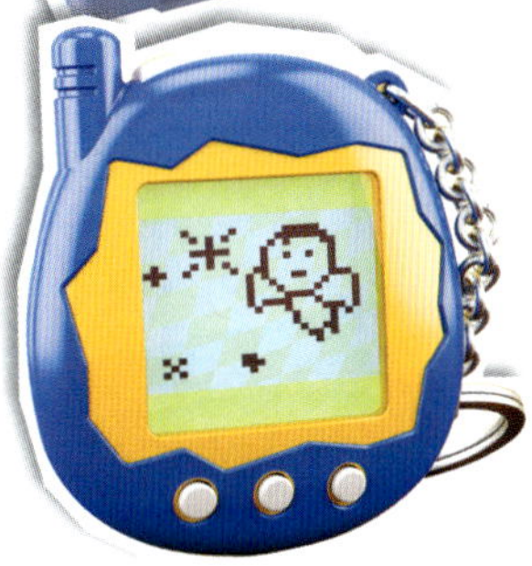

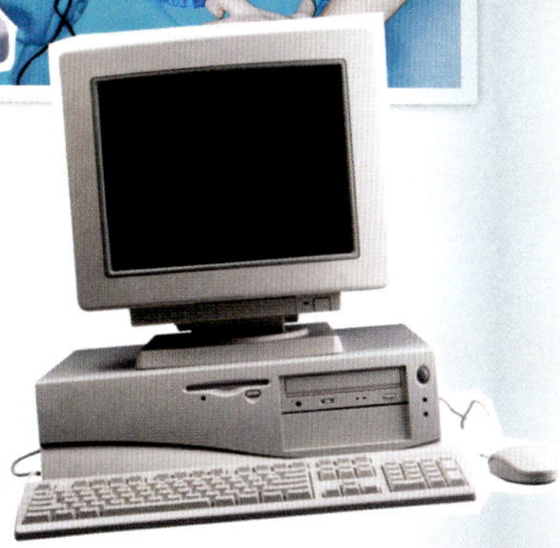

Many school subjects 25 years ago were similar to today, but classrooms were a little different. The only technology in class was a big overhead projector. Students used encyclopedias and books to find information because there was no internet. They used to write all their homework by hand and they counted the number of words in an essay. In math classes, they used calculators.

STEP 4: PRESENT

10 **Read the How to ... tips on p130. Then practice your presentation.**

11 **Peer review** **Present your poster to the class. As you listen to other students, answer the questions.**

1. Is the presentation clear and interesting?
2. What did you learn about life in the past?

2 FINAL REFLECTION

1 The task

How well can you talk about your culture in the past?

2 Super skill

Can you take turns speaking and listening when you work in groups? Give examples.

3 Language

Did you use language from the unit? Give examples.

3 Goals

WDYT?
(What do you think?)

What is your idea of success?

Vocabulary: success and achievements; word families: verbs and nouns

Grammar: past progressive; simple past and past progressive; *when* and *while*

Reading: an online article about three famous brands

Listening: a presentation about the Afghan girls' robotics team

Speaking: telling a story

Writing: a story

Project: make an infographic about a success story

Video skills p37

Real-world speaking p43

Project pp46–47

Success and achievements

1 **Work in pairs. Look at the bulletin board from Liam's bedroom. What can you say about Liam's hobbies and interests?**

2 **Match the phrases in the box to pictures 1–6 on the bulletin board.**

be famous   feel happy   get fit   learn a language   make money   win a race

3 **Complete the expressions with the verbs in exercise 2 to describe other types of achievement.**

1 ________ a prize/a competition
2 ________ something new/to surf
3 ________ a good job/good grades
4 ________ popular/rich
5 ________ friends/a difference
6 ________ part of a team/proud

4 **Complete the sentences with an expression from exercise 3.**

1 I like water sports, so I'd love to ________________ .

2 My friend was really happy to ________________ in this year's writing competition.

3 My dad says it isn't so important to ________________ on all your exams. What's important is working hard and doing your best.

4 I'm not very good at running, so I ________________ that I finished a 10k race last weekend.

5 Money isn't very important to me. I think it's more important to be happy than to ________________ .

6 My brother is studying to be a doctor because he wants to ________________ .

5 **Complete the table with achievements from exercises 2 and 3. Give reasons for your answers.**

	Achievement	Reasons
Important	*get good grades*	*study what you want*
Not important	*be rich*	*money doesn't make you happy*

6 **Work in pairs. Compare your opinions in exercise 5 with your partner.**

Do you think it's important to be rich?

No because I think that money doesn't make you happy. What do you think?

VIDEO SKILLS

7 **Watch the video. What is the vlogger's main goal? Is she successful?**

8 **Work in pairs. Discuss the questions.**

1 Why do people make 'how to' videos?

2 Why are 'how to' videos popular?

3 Why is watching a 'how to' video a good way to learn something new?

4 What could you make a 'how to' video about?

Pronunciation: Word linking p128

An online article

1 **Write the missing verbs for each group of expressions. Which ones are reasons to work for a successful company?**

1 ________ a race, a prize, a competition
2 ________ money, friends, a difference
3 ________ fit, a good job, good grades
4 ________ famous, popular, rich
5 ________ a language, something new, to surf
6 ________ part of a team, happy, proud

2 **Work in pairs. Look at the photos and discuss the questions.**

1 How many brands can you name for each of the products in the photos?
2 Do you have a favorite or least favorite brand for these products? Explain your reasons.

3 15 **Read and listen to the online article about three brands and answer the questions.**

For which brand was the key to success ...

1 making new products and doing new things?
2 old things coming back in fashion?
3 making things easy for users?

4 **Read the text again. Match the dates on the timeline with information from the text.**

▶ Subskill: Finding answers in a text

Sometimes the words in a question are different from the reading text. Look for words or phrases with a similar meaning.

5 **Complete the sentences with information from the text, using a word or phrase.**

1 The name of the app before Instagram was ...
2 25,000 people downloaded Instagram in one ...
3 Most people who first wore Vans® shoes were ...
4 Apart from making shoes, the Vans company organizes ...
5 A big problem for Polaroid® cameras was ...
6 Today some people buy instant cameras for ...

6 **Word work** **Match the definitions to the words in bold in the text. Then answer any additional questions.**

1 was in the stores for people to buy (What's the base form?) ________
2 give financial help ________
3 green, helping the planet ________
4 people who start an organization (What's the singular noun?) ________
5 from the recent past ________
6 took data from the internet onto a computer or smartphone (What's the base form?) ________

7 **Complete the sentences with the words or phrases in exercise 6.**

1 I prefer biking to going by car, because it's more ________________ .
2 People used to stand in line for hours when a new *Harry Potter* book ________________ .
3 My aunt loves fashion from the 1970s: she's really into ________________ clothes.
4 Larry Page and Sergey Brin were the ________________ of Google.
5 I ________________ that new game yesterday.
6 A lot of big companies ________________ sports teams.

CRITICAL THINKING — **SUPER SKILLS**

1 **Understand** Which of the brands in the text had the most difficulty? Why?

2 **Apply** Can you think of other difficulties businesses can have? Give some examples.

3 **Evaluate** Why do people like buying famous brands? Are brands important to you? Why/Why not?

Research

Vans holds a competition every year for high school students to design Vans shoes. Find this year's winning designs in the Van's Custom Culture Art competition.

CELEBRITY CORNER

Singer and producer Pharrell Williams works with a company called Bionic Yarn. Find out about the brand.

TIMELINE

1943

1948

1966

1960s and 70s

1980s

2010

2012

NOW

How it all started: the story of three brands

Instagram® **founders** Kevin Systrom and Mike Krieger originally launched their app as Burbn. When it proved too complicated for many users, they decided to make the app much simpler: take a nice photo, share it with your friends, comment on other people's photos. It was an instant success: on October 6, 2010, 25,000 people **downloaded** it in 24 hours. Instagram became popular really fast, but the team was very small. Just 13 people were working for Instagram when Mark Zuckerberg bought the company in 2012 for 1 billion dollars. Systrom and Krieger made a lot of money and both men are very rich today.

The Van Doren brothers started the Vans company in 1966 and their shoes were soon very popular with skateboarders. Before long, people were wearing Vans as a fashion shoe as well as for sports. The company had some financial problems in the 1980s, but soon it was doing much better. Now they make boots for snowboarders, **sponsor** sports competitions and organize an annual art competition for high school students. It's a company that also tries to make a difference, with **environmentally friendly** offices and community projects.

VANS "OFF THE WALL"

Edwin Land first had the idea of instant photography when he was traveling with his daughter in 1943, and the first Polaroid Land camera **went on sale** in 1948. They became really popular in the 1960s and 70s. But when people started to use digital cameras, the Polaroid company had a very hard time: people weren't taking photos in the same way. Today it's a different story. **Retro** things are popular again and today people are buying instant cameras to use at weddings and parties.

Polaroid

Past progressive

1 **Read the examples. Complete the table with the past progressive verbs in blue.**

> 13 people **were working** for Instagram.
> The company **was doing** very well.
> At the start of the 21st century, people **weren't taking** photos in the same way.

Affirmative/negative		
subject	***be* +*(not)***	**verb *-ing***
I, he, she, it	1 ______ / *wasn't*	3 ______
you, we, they	2 ______ / ______	

2 **Complete the sentences with the affirmative or negative form of the past progressive and the verbs in parentheses.**

1 At 6:30 am I ______________ **(sleep) (+)**.
2 Last night at 10:30 pm my dad ______________ **(make dinner) (–)**.
3 One hour ago we ______________ **(play sports) (+)**.
4 This time last week, we ______________ **(study) (–)** English.
5 Two minutes ago our teacher ______________ **(write) (+)** on the board.

3 **Work in pairs. Write true sentences starting with the time phrases in exercise 2. Compare your sentences with your partner.**

4 **Read the examples and add them to the tables.**

> **Was** the Vans company **having** problems in the 1970s? No, it **wasn't**.
> **Who was** Edwin Land **traveling** with in 1943?

Wh- questions				
question word	***be***	**subject**	**verb *-ing***	
Where	**were**	they	**going**	yesterday?

Yes/No questions			
be	**subject**	**verb *-ing***	
Were	they	**wearing**	sunglasses?
Yes/No,	**subject**	***be* (+ *not*)**	
Yes,	they	**were**.	

5 **Write questions in the past progressive.**

1 **(boy / walk)** quickly or slowly at the start?
____
2 **(what / boy / do)** while **(he / walk)** ?
____
3 **(what / birds / do)** ?
____
4 **(any other people / travel)** ?
____
5 **(how / boy / move)** in the second part?
____
6 **(who / boy / talk to)** ?
____

6 16 **Listen to a sequence of sounds and answer the questions in exercise 5.**

7 **Answer the question to solve the Brain teaser.**

BRAIN TEASER

Each suspect was carrying one thing and wearing one of the items of clothing. The police know that the bank robber was wearing a hat.

- Mark wasn't carrying a camera or a beach bag.
- Mark and Clara weren't wearing a scarf.
- Clara was wearing sunglasses.
- The person who was carrying a camera was wearing a scarf.

	Jana	Mark	Clara
backpack			
camera			
beach bag			
sunglasses			
hat			
scarf	✓	✗	✗

Can you find the identity of the bank robber?

Reinforcement and Challenge Grammar bootcamp p120

Word families: verbs and nouns

1 Read the board. Which presentation topic would you choose? Why?

Presentation homework

Prepare a three-minute presentation on one of the following topics:

- a time you decided to **compete** for a prize
- a story of an amazing **achievement**
- a person you would **invite** to speak at your school and why
- an **invention** that changed the world

Be ready to give your presentation next week.

2 Look at the words in bold in exercise 1.

1 Which are verbs, and which are nouns?
2 What are the two endings for the nouns?

3 Match 1–4 to a–d to make nouns.

1 achieve a -ion
2 invent b -ment
3 competi c -ation
4 invit d -tion

4 Complete the table with the corresponding verb or noun.

Verb	Noun
compete	1
2	invitation
3	improvement
inform	4
educate	5
6	agreement
7	advertisement

5 Work in pairs. Complete the sentence with a noun or the correct form of the verb in parentheses. Then ask and answer the questions.

1 Where do you look for ________ **(inform)** when you do your homework?
2 What's your favorite sports ________ **(compete)** ?
3 Do you think that technology ________ **(improve)** our lives? How?
4 What is your favorite ________ **(advertise)**?
5 When was the last time someone ________ **(invite)** you to a party?

A presentation

6 17 Listen to a student giving a presentation. Which topic in exercise 1 does she talk about?

7 What problems did the girls have?

Subskill: Writing notes

When you answer questions, make notes first using key words to help you remember. If necessary, write complete sentences after you finish listening.

8 Listen again and answer the questions. Write notes first.

1 How old are the girls?
2 What happened when they tried to get materials for their robot?
3 How long did they have to make their robot?
4 How many times did they go to Kabul for visas?
5 How did they get visas in the end?
6 What did the girls do when their robot broke?
7 What did the girls win?

9 Work in pairs. What do you think was the girls' greatest achievement?

Simple past and past progressive

1 Read the examples and answer the questions.

While the girls **were waiting**, they **tried** to invent a robot.
They **were practicing** with their robot when it **broke**.

1. How many actions are there in each sentence: one or two?
2. Which action is long? Which is short?
3. Which tense do we use for the long action? Which do we use for the short action?

2 Circle the correct option.

1. I **went/was going** to a robotics competition while I **stayed/was staying** in the USA.
2. We **walked/were walking** home from school, when it **started/was starting** to rain.
3. While I **visited/was visiting** my cousin, I **learned/was learning** to surf.
4. When the bus **came/was coming**, I **talked/ was talking** on the phone.
5. We **watched/were watching** when our team **won/was winning** the Cup.

when and *while*

3 Read the examples and circle the correct option in the rules.

They were practicing with their robot **when** it broke.
While they were practicing with their robot, it broke.

1. We often use **while/when** before the past progressive.
2. We often use **when/while** before the simple past.

4 Complete the sentences with the simple past or past progressive.

1. The sun ________ **(shine)** when I ________ **(wake up)** today.
2. I ________ **(call)** my friend while I ________ **(wait)** for the bus to arrive.
3. We ________ **(chat)** when our teacher ________ **(come)** into class today.
4. My parents ________ **(meet)** while they ________ **(work)** in a store.
5. My dad ________ **(make)** dinner when I ________ **(get)** home yesterday.

5 Write questions. In each question, use both the simple past and past progressive.

1. where / your parents / live / when / they / meet ?
2. what / they / do / when / you / get / up yesterday ?
3. Who / you / talk to / while / you / come / to school ?
4. What / you / do / while / you / wait / for the bus ?

6 Work in pairs. Ask and answer the questions in exercise 5.

7 Work in pairs. How many crazy sentences can you make using the prompts?

I	eat ice cream	while when	run to catch the bus
We	see a spaceship		find a million dollars
Our teacher	sing in the shower		meet [famous person]
[famous person]	step on a snake		have breakfast

8 Circle the correct option.

GRAMMAR ROUND-UP
1 2 3 4 5 6 7 8

Selena Gomez growing up

Selena Gomez is rich and famous, but her life **1 was/were** very different in the past. She used to **2 live/living** with her mother in a small apartment in Los Angeles. They **3 weren't having/didn't have** much money and they couldn't **4 buy/to buy** nice things. Selena's mother worked as an actor. That's how she **5 become/became** interested in acting.

Selena got her first job when she was nine. A few years later, she got a part in a Disney® show. Selena **6 worked/was working** on this show when she **7 met/was meeting** Justin Bieber! Now she acts and sings, and does a lot of work for charity.

A few years **8 before/ago**, Selena was ill, so now she eats a healthy diet and does exercise at least **9 twice a week/two times in a week**. She has millions of followers on Instagram. She's one of the most popular people in the world!

Telling a story

1 Watch the video. Which famous person did Diego see and where?

2 Watch again. Which Key phrases do you hear?

3 Complete the dialogue with the Key phrases. Watch again and check.

Jen Great movie! The way he climbs and jumps – it's awesome!

Diego I know. Did I ever **1** ________________ the time I saw Tom Holland?

Jen You're **2** ________________ !

Diego It's true. I was staying with my cousin in London at the time.

Jen So, **3** ________________ ?

Diego Well, we were walking in the park one day when we saw people playing sports.

Jen Right.

Diego They were free running, you know, doing acrobatics.

Jen And one of them was Tom Holland?

Diego Yeah, **4** ________________ he was training at the park.

Jen **5** ________________ ! Did you say anything to him?

Diego No, we just watched for a while. He was really good!

Jen I can't believe you actually saw Spider-Man!

4 Create your own dialogue. You can invent the story. Follow the steps in the Skills boost.

SKILLS BOOST

THINK
Work in pairs. Make notes about a time you saw a famous person.
1 Where were you? What were you doing?
2 What was (the famous person) doing?
3 What did you do? What did he/she say or do?

PREPARE
Prepare your dialogue. Remember to use the Key phrases.

PRACTICE
Practice your dialogue. Take turns telling the story.

PERFORM
Act out your dialogue for the class.

5 **Peer review** Listen to your classmates. Answer the questions.
1 Who did they meet or see? What happened?
2 Which Key phrases did they use?

Key phrases
Starting a story: Did I ever tell you about the time ...
It all started when ...

Keeping the listener interested: Can you imagine?
You'll never guess what happened.
It turns out ...

Responding: You're kidding!
So, what happened?
That's awesome/incredible/amazing/terrible!
What a nightmare!

US → UK

It's **awesome**! (US) → It's **brilliant**! (UK)

We saw people **playing sports**. (US) → We saw people **doing sport**. (UK)

One day, Billy Reid was walking along the beach near his home in Florida when he saw $100 in the sand. The 14-year-old picked up the money. Then he saw another $100, and another. Soon, he had $1,500 in his hands.

Billy, a golf fan, was with friends from a local golf organization when he found the money. They couldn't believe it when he showed it to them. Billy didn't think twice. When he saw a police officer, he gave him the money.

Billy's story was in all the newspapers and on television. A few days later, he received a phone call. It was an invitation to play video golf with some professional golf players. Billy was really happy. He played with some of his favorite players – and won! In the end, he didn't get any money, but he got a wonderful surprise.

A story

1 **Read the story from a school magazine. Choose the best title.**

- a Teen wins golf competition
- b Honest teenager gets a special surprise
- c Boy wins prize of $1,500

2 **Read the story again. Put the events in the correct order.**

- a Billy received an invitation to meet his heroes.
- b He gave the money to a police officer.
- c He showed the money to his friends.
- d People heard about his story in the news.
- e Billy found more than $1,000 in the sand.

▶ Subskill: Time expressions

Time expressions help to show the correct order of events in a story.

3 **Which time expressions can you find in the story?**

a few days later after that at the time in the end later one day soon then

4 **Circle the correct option.**

1 Later/One day, Anupriya was watching TV when she heard about floods in her country. She wanted to buy a bike **2 soon/at the time**, but she decided to donate money to victims of the flood.

3 In the end/A few days later, a reporter heard about her story and wrote about it. **4 After that/After**, other reporters told her story too. **5 At the time/Soon** she was in all the papers.

6 In the end/Then a bike company sent her a message saying that they wanted to give her a new bike every year of her life! **7 In the end/After that**, Anupriya got an amazing reward for her kindness.

5 **Write a story for the school magazine. Follow the steps in the Skills boost.**

17-year-old Miles Solomon does a physics project – he has a surprise

he checks data from the International Space Station – he finds a mistake

he checks the data again and again – he is sure

he goes to his physics teacher – they send an email to NASA

he gets a reply from NASA – they say thank you – no special prize!

he is happy – he wants to work with NASA in the future

SKILLS BOOST

THINK

Read the notes about Miles Solomon on p44. Choose a title for your story.

____

PREPARE

1 Divide the information into three paragraphs:
- The beginning of the story
- What happened next
- The result – a positive message

2 Think about where you can include time expressions in your story.

____

____

____

____

____

____

____

____

____

____

____

____

____

____

____

____

____

____

WRITE

Write your story.

One day, ...

CHECK

Read your story and answer the questions.

1 Do you include a title and three paragraphs? ☐

2 Do you use the simple past and past progressive? ☐

3 Do you use *when* and *while*? ☐

4 Do you use time expressions correctly? ☐

6 Peer review **Exchange your story with another student. Does the writer make the story interesting? How?**

Quick review

Grammar

Past progressive

Affirmative and negative

was/wasn't, were/weren't + verb *-ing*

*I **was having** dinner at seven o'clock last night.*

*Jodi **wasn't (was not) sitting** in her usual place yesterday.*

*We **were doing** math this time yesterday.*

*They **weren't (were not) wearing** a school uniform on Sunday.*

Questions and short answers

(question word) + *was/were* + subject + verb *-ing*

*What **were** you **doing** at eight o'clock last night?*

***Were** you **doing** your homework?*	*Yes, I **was**.* *No, I **wasn't**.*
***Were** your parents **watching** TV?*	*Yes, they **were**.* *No, they **weren't**.*

Simple past and past progressive

We often use the simple past and past progressive together in the same sentence.

We use the past progressive to talk about a long action and the simple past to talk about a short action that happened during that time.

*I **was taking** a shower when you **called**.*

*We **were playing** a video game when my computer **crashed**.*

when and *while*

We often use *while* before the past progressive.

We often use *when* before the simple past.

*We were playing football **when** it **started** to rain.*

*It started to rain **while** we **were playing** football.*

Vocabulary

18 Success and achievements

be famous/popular/rich
feel part of a team/happy/proud
get fit/a good job/good grades
learn a language/something new/to surf
make money/friends/a difference
win a race/a prize/a competition

19 Word families: verbs and nouns

achieve → achievement
advertise → advertisement
agree → agreement
compete → competition
educate → education
improve → improvement
inform → information
invent → invention
invite → invitation

3 Project

WDYT?
(What do you think?)

What is your idea of success?

TASK: Make an infographic about a success story, either about a person or an organization.

Learning outcomes

1 I can research and present an infographic about a success story.

2 I can take on different roles when I work in pairs or groups.

3 I can use appropriate language from the unit.

Graphic organizer → Project planner p131

1 Watch a video of students presenting their infographic. What makes Ellie's success special?

STEP 1: THINK

2 **Look at the infographic in the Model project. What information does it contain?**

- age or date of birth
- personal life
- education
- information about money
- problems or difficulties
- when and why she decided to aim for success
- achievements
- plans for the future

3 **Work in pairs. What does the infographic include that makes the information more attractive?**

photographs ...

STEP 2: PLAN

4 **Work in pairs. Choose a successful person (athlete, musician ...) or an organization you admire.**

5 **Research the person or organization.**

- Save facts and information in a document, or take notes.
- Try to find photos or other images (maps, logos, etc.).
- Organize your information into sections (e.g. family, studies) as you save it.

STEP 3: CREATE

6 **Work in pairs. Read the tips in the Super skills box and practice saying the Key phrases with your partner.**

COLLABORATION — **SUPER SKILLS**

Taking on different roles

Tips

Share the work equally between you.

Don't always work the same way. If you normally write and your partner speaks, change what you do.

Try to develop new skills.

Key phrases

OK, why don't you do X and I'll do Y?

Do you want to insert the photos?

You type and I'll read out the information.

Do you want to change, so I do the writing now?

Why don't you type this part?

7 **Work together to create your infographic. Use the list in exercise 2 to help you. Use the tips and Key phrases in the Super skills box.**

Model project

ELLIE ROBINSON

Ellie Robinson is a Paralympic® swimmer

Ellie was born in August 2001

Ellie lives in Northampton, England, with her parents Hannah and Will.

Ellie has a condition called achondroplasia. This means she is very short.

When she isn't training, Ellie likes spending time with her friends.

Ellie trains five days a week for 15 hours. She is often at the swimming pool at 5:00 am!

Ellie went to school and took exams, just like any teenager.

Ellie said, 'If I can inspire one child somewhere in the world, that's enough for me.'

MAJOR MILESTONES

Ellie was watching her hero, Ellie Simmonds, at the London Olympics when she decided to train more seriously. Ellie Simmonds also has achondroplasia.

Ellie won gold medals at the Rio Olympics and the Commonwealth Games. She was only 15.

After that, Ellie won an important prize: the BBC Young Sports Personality of the Year. She also became a Member of the British Empire and met Prince Charles.

STEP 4: PRESENT

8 Read the *How to ...* tips on p131. Then prepare to present your infographic.

9 Peer review Work with another pair. In turns, present your infographic. As you listen, answer the questions.

1 Do you find out interesting information about the person or organization?

2 Why is this a good example of a success story?

3 FINAL REFLECTION

1 The task

Is the infographic clear and attractive?

Did you give a good summary of the success story?

2 Super skill

Did you take on different roles? Give examples.

3 Language

In your infographic and explanation, did you use language from the unit? Give examples.

4 Spend!

WDYT?
(What do you think?)

How can teenagers learn about money?

Vocabulary: money; adverbs

Grammar: quantifiers; comparatives and superlatives, (*not*) *as* ... *as*

Reading: a magazine article about old toys and technology

Listening: an interview with the founder of a skills-sharing service

Speaking: giving advice

Writing: notes and messages

Project: make a proposal for a business idea

Video skills p49

Real-world speaking p55

Project pp58–59

Money

1 **Look at the words in the box. Which can you see in the photos?**

allowance bank notes bill cash coins
credit card discount price receipt wallet

2 **Work in pairs. Answer the questions about the pictures.**

1 Which country are the bank notes from?
2 How many coins can you see?
3 What's the price of the flip flops?
4 Where do you think the bill is from?
5 How much is the discount?

What about question one?

I don't know, it's difficult to see. I think the bank notes are from the USA. What do you think?

Yes, they're dollars!

The Money Quiz

Are you good with money? Take our quiz and find out.

1 You win $1,000 in a competition. What do you do? ☐
a spend all the money on clothes and having fun
b put it in the bank and save it

2 You'd like to buy a bike, but it costs a lot of money. What do you do? ☐
a offer to do chores at home to earn the money
b ask your parents to pay for it

3 Your friend wants to borrow money from you. What do you do? ☐
a say yes – you often lend money to your friends
b say no – money is important and you don't want to waste it

4 Your grandparents give you a video game for your birthday, but you already have it. What do you do? ☐
a swap it for a different game
b sell it at a discount and buy another one

Find your score

1 a – 1 point, b – 3 points
2 a – 3 points, b – 1 point
3 a – 1 point, b – 3 points
4 a – 3 points, b – 1 point

8–12 points: You're good with money – good job!

4–6 points: You aren't very good with money. Perhaps you need to be more careful?

3 Circle the correct option.

1 Some teenagers get **allowance/coins** every week from their parents.
2 After a meal in a restaurant, you ask for the **receipt/bill**.
3 People pay with a credit card when they don't have any **cash/wallet**.
4 When you pay less than normal, you get a **price/discount**.
5 After you pay, a salesperson gives you a **receipt/bill**.

4 Work in pairs. Discuss the questions.

1 How many types of coins are there in your country? What bank notes are there?
2 Do teenagers in your country get an allowance?
3 Do your parents usually pay with a credit card or cash?

5 Read the quiz but don't answer! Match some of the verbs in red with definitions 1–8.

1 get money for work that you do
2 get something as a prize in a competition
3 exchange, give one thing and receive another thing
4 keep something to use later
5 ask for something to use that you give back later
6 use something badly
7 give something to someone to use for a short time
8 give something to another person in return for money

6 Take the quiz. Then calculate your score. Do you agree with the results?

Learning words in pairs

It's sometimes a good idea to think of words in pairs. This can help you to remember the difference between the two words. For example, *earn/win*.

7 Work in pairs. Explain the difference between the words.

1 earn/win
2 swap/sell
3 borrow/lend
4 spend/waste
5 pay/buy

VIDEO SKILLS

8 Watch the video. What food do you see?

9 Work in pairs. Discuss the questions.

1 Why are vloggers popular?
2 What is there in the video that helps you to understand it? Think about images, animations and the presenter.
3 Would you like to be a vlogger? Why/Why not?

A magazine article

1 **Work in pairs. Discuss the questions.**

1 What do you usually spend money on?
2 Are you saving for anything right now? What do you want to buy?
3 What is a good way for teenagers to earn money in your country?
4 Do you ever buy or sell things online? What websites do you use?

2 **Look at the photos in the article. What can you see? Do you have any of these at home?**

3 20 **Read and listen to the article. Which of these does it mention?**

a things that you can sell online
b how much money people pay for different things
c instructions about how to sell old objects online

▶ Subskill: Scanning

When you read for information about numbers, don't read the whole article in detail. Scan the text and look for the numbers. Then read the information that relates to the numbers.

4 **Find the answers to the questions. (You have one minute!)**

1 What did someone buy for $360? ________
2 What is worth $400? ________
3 How much could you get for an old phone? ________
4 What's the most expensive object in the article? ________
5 How much did someone pay for an empty cereal box? ________

5 **Are the sentences true, false or is there no information? Give reasons for your answer.**

1 There is a website where you can buy and sell a type of toy.
2 You can sell any piece of LEGO© for $200.
3 Happy Meal® toys from Japan are more popular than other toys.
4 You can sell recent cell phones for a lot of money.
5 People ate a lot of cereals in the 80s and 90s.
6 Some people collect old boxes of cereal.

6 **Word work** **Match the definitions to the words in bold in the text.**

1 this describes something that costs a lot or is important to a person ________
2 a group of things of the same type ________
3 a type of breakfast food that we usually eat with milk ________
4 a person who collects a particular type of thing as a hobby ________
5 a collection of expensive objects, possibly made of gold or silver ________
6 this describes how much people will pay to buy something ________

7 **Complete the sentences with words from exercise 6.**

1 They found ________ when they opened the Egyptian pyramids.
2 I usually have toast for breakfast, but I sometimes have ________ .
3 My cousin is a ________ of old coins. He has hundreds.
4 My uncle has a complete ________ of Pokémon™ cards.
5 These old books are probably ________ a lot of money now.
6 The most ________ things I have are my laptop and phone.

CRITICAL THINKING — SUPER SKILLS

1 **Remember** What information in the article do you think is most surprising?
2 **Analyze** What are the advantages and disadvantages of buying things online? (Think of at least two advantages and two disadvantages.)
3 **Evaluate** In your opinion, is it better to shop online or go to a normal store?

Research

Go online and find the price for an old game or toy that you have. What is the most expensive old game or toy you can find?

CELEBRITY CORNER

Ed Sheeran sold his childhood Lego set and raised over £4,000 for charity. Which other stars donated items to charity?

MONEY FOR YOUR OLD THINGS

Do you keep old toys and technology? Do you have too many games? If the answer is yes, try selling them online. You could make some money!

Most of us have some LEGO at home. Now, people pay a lot of money for just one piece. There's a website called www.BrickLink.com where you can sell your old LEGO pieces. A normal piece, if it's the right color, can sell for $200, and a red Darth Vader® helmet sells for $400. There aren't many original *Star Wars* Millennium Falcon sets in the world, so one of these is **worth** $12,000!

Did you use to collect Happy Meal Toys? They're free when you buy a Happy Meal at McDonald's®. Someone recently paid $360 for a **set** of the *Minions*® and one Pikachu® from a Japanese Happy Meal sold for $100! If you don't have a complete set, don't worry. You can still get about $500 for a box of mixed toys.

'A piece of LEGO can sell for $200'

FUN FACTS

Toys are more valuable in a box, so people often buy empty boxes. A box for a Yoda toy from Star Wars™ recently sold for an incredible $1,136.

Maybe you have some old boxes of **cereal** too. There were cereals for every movie character and video game in the 80s and 90s, and Nintendo cereals were especially popular. A **collector** recently paid $200 for a box of these cereals – and someone paid half that for an empty box!

These days, people change their phone every year or two, so you probably have one of these. It isn't worth much now, but don't throw it away. It could be **valuable** in the future. A 1983 Motorola® recently sold for $550, and other old phones are worth the same.

So, if you want to buy new things and you don't have enough money, go and look in your cupboard. Maybe you'll find some **treasure** there!

Quantifiers: *a lot of (lots of)*, *some*, *any*, *not much/many*

1 Read the examples. Complete the rules.

A lot of people buy and sell things online these days.
There aren't many original Star Wars sets.
Maybe you have some cereal boxes.
Do you have any Happy Meal toys?
Your phone isn't worth much money now.

We use **1** ________ and *lots of* to talk about a big number or quantity.
We use *not* **2** ________ and *not* **3** ________ to talk about a small number or quantity.
We use *not* **4** ________ with countable nouns and *not* **5** ________ with uncountable nouns.
We use *some* in affirmative sentences and **6** ________ in negative sentences and questions.

2 Circle the option which isn't correct.

1 I have **lots of/some/any** old toys at home.
2 She doesn't spend **much/many/any** time shopping.
3 There aren't **many/some/a lot of** old things in my cupboard.
4 I don't get **many/much/a lot of** allowance.
5 Do you buy **any/lots of/much** clothes online?

too much/many, (not) enough

3 Read the examples. Answer the questions.

Someone paid $1,136 for an empty box. That's too much money!
Do you have too many old toys?
You don't have enough money to buy something.
You have enough games. You don't need more!

Which quantifiers mean ... ?
1 more than necessary ________
2 less than we want ________
3 the right amount or number ________

4 Match 1–3 to a–c to make rules.

1 After *too much*, we use
2 After *too many*, we use
3 After *(not) enough*, we use

a both countable and uncountable nouns.
b an uncountable noun.
c a countable noun.

5 Complete the sentences with *too much/many* or *enough*.

1 You can't buy those expensive jeans. You don't have ________ money.
2 There are ________ people on the bus. You can't sit down.
3 People eat ________ fast food. It's so unhealthy!
4 There are 25 people and we only have 20 chairs. There aren't ________ chairs!
5 The movie starts in 20 minutes. We have ________ time to buy popcorn.

6 Circle the correct option.

NEW-STYLE STORES

1 A lot of/Much people now choose to shop online. When customers go to stores, they don't spend **2 much/many** time there, and stores are closing because they don't make **3 enough/many** money.

4 Some/Any stores are looking for new ways to find customers. One sports store in London has a skate park. Customers don't need to spend **5 enough/any** money to use it, but they often buy new sneakers while they're there.

There aren't **6 much/many** stores like this, but Toms, the shoe company, has comfortable chairs, free WiFi and a café. Now, it's easy to spend **7 too much/enough** time and money in the store!

7 Answer the question to solve the Brain teaser.

BRAIN TEASER

Adam and Ben go shopping. Adam has $20 and Ben has $50. Adam buys two T-shirts and spends $9.20. Ben buys five of the same T-shirts and a sweater. The sweater costs $20. The friends then go for lunch. A sandwich is $4 and Ben offers to pay for them both.

Does Ben have enough money?

Reinforcement and Challenge Grammar bootcamp pp121–122

Adverbs

1 **Look at the website. Why is Skills Bank 'the money-free helping system'?**

SKILLS BANK: the money-free helping system

What is Skills Bank?

With Skills Bank you can do things easily and cheaply – very cheaply! Because with Skills Bank you offer to swap your skills with people who can do different things. And it's all free. You give an hour of your time and you get an hour from someone else.

How does it work?

Imagine you have a guitar but you can't play it well. But you can speak Italian perfectly. On the website, you can offer to help people with Italian and you can find someone who can help you learn to play the guitar. Look at some skills on offer:

baking | computers | babysitting | car repairs
cleaning | piano | driving | dog-walking
gardening | guitar | languages | shopping

How do I start?

Step 1: Complete this form

I can help with Any

I need help with Any

2 ***Cheaply* is an adverb. Find three more adverbs in the text. Which one is irregular?**

3 **Complete the table with the adverbs in exercise 2.**

		adjective	adverb
most adjectives	add *-ly*		
adjectives ending in *y*	change to *-ily*		
adjectives ending in *l*	change to *-lly*	*careful*	*carefully*
irregular	–		

4 **Make adverbs from the adjectives in the box and add them to the table in exercise 3.**

amazing angry bad beautiful
clear happy hard quick slow

5 **Circle the correct option.**

1 What's the matter with Britta? She was yelling very **beautifully/angrily** at her sister.
2 It's possible to travel **quickly/cheaply** if you go camping or stay in a youth hostel.
3 Can you come **quickly/slowly** and help me? I'm making a cake, but something's not right!
4 I'm a little confused about our homework; the teacher didn't explain it very **clearly/beautifully**.
5 I'm studying very **hard/easily** right now because my exams start next week.

An interview

6 21 **Listen to part of a radio show about another skills-sharing service and circle the best description.**

Generation Skill Share is a service to …

a generate money to help older people.
b get people of different ages to help each other.
c get school children helping older people.

Subskill: Choosing between options

When you need to choose between similar options, don't decide the answer too quickly. Listen to all the information in detail before you choose.

7 **Listen again and circle the correct option.**

1 Cynthia Jackson …
   a had the idea to start Generation Skill Share.
   b needed help with her computer.
2 Cynthia's father …
   a was the first person to use Generation Skill Share.
   b would like some help using his computer.
3 Hazel Clark …
   a is 80.
   b knows more about technology now.
4 Lewis Freeman …
   a used to eat in restaurants because he couldn't cook.
   b says young people can learn more things from older people.

8 **Work in pairs. Imagine you want to use a skills-sharing service. Complete the sentences. Then compare with a partner.**

1 I can help with ______________________
2 I need help with ______________________

Comparative and superlative adjectives

1 Read the examples. Complete the rules and add examples of comparative and superlative forms.

My generation can learn from **older** people.
The Generation Skill Share service is **bigger** than it was last year
Hazel's **the best** teacher I know.
I'm **happier** with Lewis.
Things today are becoming **more expensive**.

1 For one-syllable adjectives: add *-er / -est*
older → the oldest
2 For one-syllable adjectives ending consonant + vowel + consonant: double final consonant and add ______________
3 For adjectives ending *-y*: remove ______________ and add ______________
4 For adjectives with two or more syllables: ______________
5 Some adjectives are irregular: ______________

2 Complete the sentences with the comparative or superlative forms of the adjectives in parentheses.

1 Manchester is (...) **(expensive)** than Glasgow, but London is (...) **(expensive)** city in the UK.
2 I love this noodle bar. The food is (...) **(healthy)** than other types of restaurants and it's (...) **(cheap)** place to eat around here.
3 For me, the shopping center is (...) **(bad)** place for shopping. It has (...) **(big)** stores than in town, but they're too busy and unfriendly.
4 My grandmother always says some people are (...) **(rich)** than her and some people are (...) **(poor)** than her, but (...) **(important)** thing is that she is (...) **(happy)** person in the world!

(*not*) *as* + adjective + *as*

3 Circle the option that is true about each sentence.

1 Houston is as expensive as Kansas City.
  a One city is more expensive than the other.
  b The two cities are both expensive and the prices are very similar.
2 It isn't as difficult as I thought.
  a It's less difficult than I thought.
  b It's more difficult than I thought.

4 Rewrite the sentences using (*not*) *as* + adjective + *as*.

1 Jin and Liam are equally tall. *Jin is as tall as Liam.*
2 A cell phone is less expensive than a computer.
3 Math and physics are equally difficult.
4 My bedroom is less clean than the living room.
5 Today and yesterday are equally cold.
6 Playing video games is less exciting than playing sports.

5 Circle the correct option.

GRAMMAR ROUND-UP
1 2 3 4 5 6 7 8

Was money always bank notes and coins?

No, it **1 didn't/wasn't**. In the past people used **2 lots of/much** different things as money, including cows, fish and tea! In Ancient Rome, they **3 did pay/used to pay** soldiers in salt (the English word 'salary' **4 comes/is coming** from the Latin 'salarium') and on the Pacific island of Yap they used enormous stones for money. Why did this **5 happen/happened**?

Travelers from Yap **6 explored/were exploring** another island **7 when/while** they found a new type of stone and brought it back home. These stones became their money.

However, there was a problem: the stones were **8 as big as/bigger as** a man. The people on Yap **9 couldn't to/couldn't** move them, so they decided to leave the stones in the same place. If a person paid for something with a stone, the stone didn't move, but everyone knew that it now belonged to a different person.

Reinforcement and Challenge Grammar bootcamp p122
Pronunciation: Weak forms p128

Giving advice

1 **Work in pairs. Look at the photos and discuss what possible problem there could be.**

2 **Watch the video. What solutions does Ross provide to Hannah's problem?**

3 **Watch again. Which Key phrases do you hear?**

4 **Complete the dialogue with the Key phrases. Watch again and check.**

Hannah Hi, Ross.

Ross Hi, Hannah. What's up?

Hannah I really want to buy a new skateboard, but I haven't got enough money.

Ross **1** ______________ ask your mum to buy it for you?

Hannah That's **2** ______________ . She spent a lot of money on my new guitar last week.

Ross **3** ______________ to save the money?

Hannah How could I **4** ______________ ?

Ross **5** ______________ walk home from school instead of getting the bus.

Hannah That's **6** ______________ .

Ross And it's your birthday next month, so you could ask for money instead of presents.

Hannah Thanks, I'll **7** ______________ . Cheers!

5 **Create your own dialogue. Follow the steps in the Skills boost.**

SKILLS BOOST

THINK

In pairs, think of ...

- something you would like to buy but don't have enough money for.
- ways you could get the money you need.

PREPARE

Prepare a dialogue. Remember to include phrases to give and respond to advice.

PRACTICE

Practice your dialogue.

PERFORM

Act out your dialogue for the class.

6 **Peer review** **Listen to your classmates and answer the questions.**

1. Which Key phrases do they use?
2. Do you think their plan to get money will work? Why/Why not?

Key phrases

Giving advice: Why don't you (ask) ... ?
What about (trying) ... ?
You could always (ask) ...
You should (give) ...

Asking for clarification: How could I do that?
Do you think ... ?

Accepting/rejecting advice: That's a good/great idea.
Thanks, I'll try that.
That's not going to work.
I don't think that I could do that.

UK → US

getting the bus (UK) → **taking** the bus (US)

A

Remember I lent you $10 3 WEEKS AGO??!!!! 😩 Can you pay me back? I'm going to the 🎬 tomorrow night with Bea and Lorna and I need $$$$$$ ❤️

B

Hi ________,
Mr. Harrison told us today that the school trip costs $40. I need to pay it tomorrow, so can you give me the money in the morning? Hope it's not too late.
Thanks,
Lola xx

C

To: Sent

Dear ________,

I looked at that bag that you asked me to get for Maxine's birthday; it was $45. Is that too expensive? There was a cheaper bag, but it wasn't big enough for her computer.

Lots of love,

Lola

Notes write to:

- ☐ Grandma about Maxine's present
- ☐ Maxine about the money that she borrowed
- ☐ Mom about money for museum visit

1 MESSAGE
Dear Lola,
Please get the bag you saw. No problem about the price, that's fine. I'll give you $10 extra when I see you on the weekend.
Many thanks,
________ now

2 MESSAGE
Hi darling,
No problem. I went to the bank on the way home, so I can give you the money at breakfast.
________ 1m ago

3 MESSAGE
Hey big sis,
I have your money. Sorry I forgot before. You are the best bank I know!! PS Can I borrow your black dress on Friday? Mine isn't dressy enough for the concert.
________ 2m ago

Notes and messages

1 **Lola is writing messages about money. Look at the list of people she needs to contact, then read messages A–C and add the missing names.**

2 **Read replies 1–3 that Lola received. Who wrote each one?**

3 **Read the messages again and find the following:**

- three ways to greet someone at the start of a message (Which is the most formal and which is the most informal?)
- two ways to say 'thank you'

▶ Subskill: *too* + adjective, *not* + adjective + *enough*

We use *too* + adjective when there is more than we need. *It's too hot in here.*

We use *not* + adjective + *enough* when there is insufficient of something. *He isn't fast enough for the track and field team.*

4 **Find sentences with *too* + adjective and *not* + adjective + *enough* in the messages.**

5 **Rewrite the sentences so they have the same meaning using opposite adjectives.**

1 It's too cold. *It isn't hot enough.*
2 You can't have this phone: it's too expensive.
3 The bus isn't quick enough. We'll go by train.
4 My brother is too young to see that movie.
5 These shoes aren't big enough for my feet.

6 **Write some messages. Follow the steps in the Skills boost.**

SKILLS BOOST

THINK

Think of three messages you might need to write about money to three different people. Use the ideas here or think of your own. Make notes.

- You need to pay for something at school; ask your parents for some money.
- You can't go to the stores today; ask someone to buy something for you.
- You're buying a present together with another person; leave a note about the present.

____
____
____
____
____
____
____
____
____
____
____
____
____

PREPARE

Write your messages on three separate pieces of paper.

1 Use the examples in exercise 1 to help you.
2 Include some sentences with *too* + adjective or *not* + adjective + *enough*.

WRITE

Give your messages to three different students. Write replies to the messages you receive and give them back to the student. Use the examples in exercise 2 to help you.

CHECK

Read your messages and answer the questions.

1 Do you use *too* + adjective or *not* + adjective + *enough*? ☐
2 Are the messages clear? ☐
3 Do you use the right language (more or less formal) for each person? ☐

7 **Peer review** **Look at all the messages you have. Are the messages and replies clear?**

Quick review

Grammar

Quantifiers: *a lot of (lots of), some, any, not much/many*

Use *a lot of/lots of* with countable and uncountable nouns to talk about a big number or quantity.
Use *some* in affirmative sentences and *any* in questions and negatives with countable and uncountable nouns.
*I save **a lot of money.** Do you save **any money**?*
*I try to save **some**. I **don't** spend **any money** on clothes.*
Use *not much* for a small quantity of uncountable things and *not many* for a small number of countable things.
*I **don't** have **much time**. There aren't **many people**.*

too much/many, (not) enough

Use *too much* with uncountable nouns and *too many* with countable nouns to talk about an excess.
*There are **too many spelling mistakes** in this exercise.*
Use *enough* to say you have the necessary amount and *not enough* to say you have less than necessary.
*I **don't** have **enough money** for the shoes.*

Comparatives and superlatives

To compare two things, use comparative adjective + *than*.
To compare three things, use *the* + superlative adjective.
*Boston is **more expensive than** Seattle. New York is **the most expensive** city in the USA.*

1 One-syllable adjectives → + *-er*, *-est* or + *-r*, *-st* if the adjective finishes in *-e*
*old – old**er** – the old**est*** *white – white**r** – the white**st***
2 One-syllable adjectives ending in vowel + consonant → double the final consonant + *-er*, *-est*
*fat – fa**tter** – the fa**ttest***
3 Adjectives ending in *-y* → ~~y~~ + *-ier*, *-iest*
*sunny – sunn**ier** – the sunn**iest***
4 Adjectives with two or more syllables → *more*, *the most* + adjective
*difficult – **more** difficult – **the most** difficult*
5 *good – better – the best* *bad – worse – the worst*

Comparing with *(not) as* + adjective + *as*

To say things are the same use *as* + adjective + *as*
To say one thing is less than the other use *not as* + adjective + *as*
*My brother is **as tall as** me. My sister is **not as tall as** me.*

Vocabulary

22 Money

allowance, bank notes, bill, borrow, buy, cash, coins, cost, credit card, discount, earn, lend, pay, price, receipt, save, sell, spend, swap, wallet, waste, win

23 Adverbs

amazingly, angrily, badly, beautifully, carefully, cheaply, clearly, easily, happily, hard, perfectly, quickly, slowly, well

4 Project

WDYT?
(What do you think?)

How can teenagers learn about money?

TASK: Make a proposal to get money for a business idea.

Learning outcomes

1 I can create and present an idea for a new business.

2 I can communicate effectively in a presentation.

3 I can use appropriate language from the unit.

Graphic organizer → Project planner p131

1 Watch a video of students presenting their idea. What is the money-making idea?

STEP 1: THINK

2 **Match a–f with the slides in the Model project.**

- **a** how the idea can help people
- **b** how to tell people about the idea
- **c** the problem it can solve
- **d** the money you need and why
- **e** who the idea can help
- **f** the name

3 **Are the sentences true or false?**

1 There is a lot of information on each slide.
2 There is one picture on each slide.
3 There are long sentences.
4 There is only one color on all the slides.
5 There is a question on some slides.

STEP 2: PLAN

4 **Work in pairs. Think of an idea for your business. It can be:**

- something you do (take photos, plan parties, etc.)
- something you make (cakes, T-shirts, etc.)

5 **Make notes for your business. Consider each of the points in Step 1.**

STEP 3: CREATE

6 **Read the *How to ...* tips on p131. Then work together to create your presentation. Use the Model project to help you.**

7 **Work in pairs. Read the tips in the Super skills box and practice saying the Key phrases with your partner.**

COMMUNICATION — **SUPER SKILLS**

Communicating effectively in a formal situation to a group

Tips

Remember who you are speaking to and adapt the way you speak if you need to.

Show that you are confident; look at everyone; speak loudly; don't speak too fast.

Use gestures and smile.

Key phrases

Do you think we should be serious or funny? Perhaps I could tell a personal story?

Remember, this is a business meeting.

I think we should speak clearly.

How can we show that we're confident?

We mustn't be nervous.

8 **Work in pairs. Prepare to give your presentation. Use the tips and Key phrases in the Super skills box.**

Grammar and Vocabulary Quick review p57

Model project

FILE EDIT VIEW INSERT

Slide 1

iFixphone

Slide 2

We all love our phones ...,
but we sometimes break them!

What do we do?

Throw them away: bad for the environment

Buy a new one: very expensive!

Slide 3

We can fix your phone!

Slide 4

We can help:

everybody!

students

parents

older people

Slide 5

Advertisements:

posters at school

webpage

social media

Slide 6

We need:

$500 – for materials, training and advertisements

To solve all your phone problems!

STEP 4: PRESENT

9 Peer review **Present your business idea to the class. As you listen to your classmates, think about the questions.**

1 Do you think that each business can make money? Give reasons for your answer.

2 Which business do you want to be part of?

4 FINAL REFLECTION

1 The task

Did you find a good idea for a business?

How successful was your presentation? Give examples.

2 Super skill

Did you communicate effectively to your audience? Give examples.

3 Language

In your slides and presentation, did you use language from the unit? Give examples.

5 A better place

WDYT?
(What do you think?)

How can we improve our environment?

Vocabulary: rooms and furniture; your environment

Grammar: *will* for predictions; *might*; first and zero conditional

Reading: a newspaper report about 3D home printing

Listening: a podcast about environment campaigners

Speaking: making decisions

Writing: an advertisement

Project: conduct a green audit of your school and make proposals for change

Video skills p61

Real-world speaking p67

Project pp70–71

Rooms and furniture

1 Look at the plan of a house. Complete the words with vowels to make rooms.

1 B A THR O O M	4 H __ LL	7 __ FF __ C __
2 B __ DR __ __ M	5 K __ TCH __ N	8 ST __ __ RS
3 G __ R __ G __	6 L __ V __ NG R __ __ M	9 Y __ RD

2 Match the words in the box with items of furniture A–M.

armchair basin ~~bookshelf~~ carpet closet couch cupboard curtains fridge oven sink trash can washing machine

3 **Complete the list in exercise 2 with the room in which you would find the items of furniture.**

bookshelf – A – office, living room, bedroom

4 **Work in pairs. Categorize the vocabulary in a different way.**

Categorizing vocabulary

Categorizing is a good way to study vocabulary. As well as categorizing the words by room, try categorizing by use (e.g. things you can sit on), color (e.g. things which are white) or qualities (e.g. things with doors).

What about things with doors?

OK, oven, closet, fridge ...

5 **Complete the sentences with a room or an item of furniture.**

The **1** ________ is under the window in the **2** ________ , so I can see the yard while I'm doing the dishes.

I often wake up early because the **3** ________ in my **4** ________ are very thin and it gets very light.

My favorite place to read is sitting in the big **5** ________ next to the couch in the **6** ________ or lying on the **7** ________ on the floor.

My mom's a translator and she works from home. She has an **8** ________ with a desk for her computer. There's a **9** ________ for trash under the desk and a **10** ________ for all her dictionaries.

6 **Work in pairs. Draw a plan of your home, with furniture and other items. Then describe two of the rooms to your partner.**

My bathroom isn't very big. There's a shower, toilet and a small trash can, and it has a basin with a mirror where we wash, comb our hair and brush our teeth.

VIDEO SKILLS

7 **Work in pairs. Watch the video and answer the questions.**

1 Why is the video called 'The nomadic life'?
2 What kind of video is this?
3 What do you think the message of the video is?
4 Who would you recommend this video to?

A newspaper report

1 **Work in pairs. Look at the photos on pp62–63 and answer the questions.**

1 What connects the photos?

2 How do the photos connect to the title of the text?

2 **Read the text quickly and check your answer in exercise 1.**

Subskill: Reading quickly

When reading quickly, try to focus on understanding the general idea. Don't stop when you see a word you don't know.

3 **Four headings are missing from the text. Match questions a–e with paragraphs 1–4. There is one question you don't need.**

a What's happening in the Netherlands?

b How will 3D printing change things in the future?

c What problems are there with 3D printing?

d How did 3D printing start?

e What are the advantages of building with 3D printing?

4 24 **Read and listen to the text. Find phrases with the same meaning as sentences 1–7.**

1 It costs a lot to build a normal house.

Building a house is often a very long and expensive job.

2 Chuck Hull invented 3D printing more than 30 years ago.

3 Russian experts took one day to build a house.

4 3D houses don't take as long to make.

5 Many normal houses aren't as good in bad weather.

6 The houses in the Netherlands will probably be ready next year.

7 A 3D space station could open in the future.

5 **Work in pairs. What can you remember about the text? Try to answer the questions in exercise 3 in your own words.**

6 Word work **Match the definitions to the words in bold in the text.**

1 a level in a building ________

2 used again, often to make something different ________

3 people who design houses and buildings ________

4 place where astronauts work ________

5 countries where people have less money and fewer public services ________

6 the physical forms of things ________

7 **Complete the sentences with words from exercise 6. Change the form if necessary.**

1 The ________ Frank Gehry designed the Guggenheim Museum in Bilbao, Spain. He also designed a hat for Lady Gaga.

2 We can use ________ plastic bottles to make T-shirts, sweaters and carpets.

3 A ________ with 16 sides is called a hexakaidecagon.

4 With a population of 28 million, Jabodetabek in Indonesia is one of the biggest cities in ________ .

5 The Burj Khalifa is one of the tallest buildings in the world. It has over 160 ________ .

6 The International ________ travels at 27,724 km per hour.

CRITICAL THINKING — SUPER SKILLS

1 **Remember** What were the advantages of using 3D printing?

2 **Evaluate** Can you think of any disadvantages of this change in building?

3 **Create** Imagine you can build your own 3D home. What does it look like?

CELEBRITY CORNER

Adele's house in England is eco-friendly because it has solar panels. Find another celebrity with an eco-friendly house.

Print your own home

Building a house is often a very long and expensive job. But this might change in the next few years. The reason? 3D printing.

1 __

American engineer Chuck Hull introduced 3D printing in 1986. Now we can build many different things using 3D technology, including bridges and buildings.

2 __

It's quick: in Russia they built one house in just 24 hours. This means it's a very good way to build houses to help people in an emergency situation.

It's more environmentally friendly: you can make 3D houses from **recycled** materials.

It's cheap: Chinese company Winsun says 3D houses use 60% fewer materials and 70% less time than traditional buildings.

It's strong: 3D houses are better in a strong wind than many normal houses.

3 __

In the Netherlands, the **architects** at Van Wijnen are working on what they say are the first 3D printed houses that people will actually be able to live in.

The houses will have unusual **shapes**. The first house will be on one **floor**: it won't have any stairs. The other houses will be bigger, with more floors and several bedrooms. If everything goes to plan, people will move into the houses next year. Many people think this will completely change the way we build houses.

4 __

In the future, people will be able to design their own personalized homes much more cheaply. And some organizations, like charity New Story, think 3D printing might help with housing problems in **the developing world**. But 3D technology could also be important in space. The European Space Agency is working on a 3D-printed **space station** and NASA is planning to use 3D technology to build on Mars.

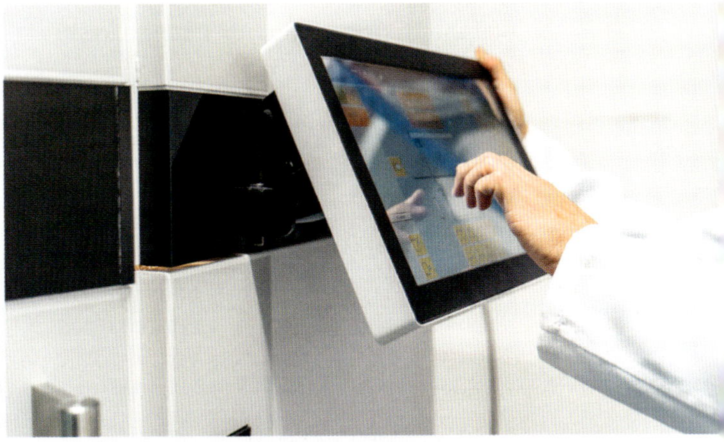

will for predictions: affirmative and negative

1 Read the examples and complete the table.

Houses **will** have unusual shapes.
The house **won't** have any stairs.

Affirmative/negative			
subject	***will/ won't***	**verb**	
Houses	________	________	unusual shapes.
The house	________	________	any stairs.

2 Complete the text about homes in the future with the positive or negative form of the verbs.

Houses in the future **1** ________ **(be –)** the same as homes today. There **2** ________ **(be +)** cameras outside the house and you **3** ________ **(use –)** a key to open the door. The temperature **4** ________ **(change +)** automatically and people **5** ________ **(need –)** to do housework: robots **6** ________ **(do +)** it!

will for predictions: questions

3 Read the examples and complete the tables.

How **will** 3D printing change things in the future?
Will they use 3D printing in space? Yes, they **will**.

Wh- questions			
***Wh-* word**	***will***	**subject**	**verb?**
How		3D printing	________ things?

Yes/No questions and short answers		
Will	**subject**	**verb?**
	they	________ 3D printing in space?
Yes/No,	**subject**	***will/won't***
No,		

4 How will the things in the box change in 20 years? Write them in the table.

beds exams food houses kitchens school sports transportation TV

The same	Won't exist	Different
		houses – 3D printed houses

5 Work in pairs. Compare your ideas in exercise 4.

6 How will your life be different when you're 30? Order the words to make questions.

1 will / your job / be / what ?
____
2 a car / will / have / you ?
____
3 will / you / where / live ?
____
4 on vacation / where / you / will / go ?
____
5 will / how / free time / spend / you / your ?
____

might

7 Look at the examples and circle the correct option to complete the rules.

The houses **will** have unusual shapes.
3D printing **might** help with housing problems.

1 ***will/might*** means something is definite in the future.
2 ***will/might*** means something is a possibility.

8 Circle the correct option.

1 Jan **will/might** be 15 next year. (He's 14 now.)
2 It **will/might** be sunny tomorrow. (It's the middle of the summer in Spain.)
3 It **will/might** be sunny tomorrow. (It's early spring in Canada.)
4 Tomorrow **will/might** be Monday. (Today is Sunday.)

9 Work in pairs. Discuss your answers to the questions in exercise 6. Use *will* and *might*.

When you're 30, what will your job be?

I don't know. I might be a pilot!

10 Answer the question to solve the Brain teaser.

BRAIN TEASER

Tess is 14 and her sister Vera is half her age.

How old will Vera be when Tess is twice her present age?

Reinforcement and Challenge Grammar bootcamp p123

Your environment

1 **Read the tips. Which things do you do to make the environment better?**

Ways to make your environment a better place

1 Walk or ride your bike to school. Cars are one of the main causes of air **pollution**.
2 Remember to turn off your computer when you aren't using it.
3 Give up using plastic. Plastic kills over a million sea birds and animals every year.
4 **Recycle** your **waste**. Take paper, glass and plastic to the **recycling bins**.
5 Don't turn up your heat in the winter. Wear a sweater instead.
6 **Plant** a tree. Trees help to **reduce** CO_2, but we cut down about 15 billion trees a year.
7 **Reuse** things that you normally throw away. Use old boxes for shelves and put flowers in bottles.
8 Pick up paper, bottles and cans that you see in the street and park. **Trash** can kill wildlife.

2 **Look at the words in bold in exercise 1. Match the words with definitions 1–8.**

1 the material that we don't need
2 put (trees, flowers) in the ground
3 use again
4 paper, bottles, etc. people throw on the ground
5 the dangerous material in water and in air
6 make less
7 the place to put paper, plastic, etc.
8 change materials like paper or plastic to use again

3 **Find six of the phrasal verbs in the box in the tips. Explain the meaning of each one.**

cut down give up pick up throw away turn down turn off turn on turn up

4 **Complete the sentences with phrasal verbs. Which sentences are true for you?**

1 I ________ my computer when I'm not using it.
2 I never ________ old clothes. I recycle them.
3 I decided to ________ using plastic straws. They're bad for the environment.
4 I always ________ cola cans when I see them, and I put them in the recycling bin.
5 When it's warm, I open the windows. I don't ________ the air conditioning.

A podcast

5 25 **Listen to a podcast about campaigners for the environment. What does each campaign want people to do?**

Subskill: Answering true, false and no information questions

The first time you listen, try to answer the questions that you are sure of. The second time you listen, focus on the other sentences. If you don't hear the facts, mark your answer as 'no information'.

6 **Listen again. Are the sentences true, false or is there no information?**

1 Patrick explains why trees are important for the planet.
2 Felix started the campaign because they cut down trees in his area.
3 He wants to plant one trillion trees in the next 50 years.
4 Nadia picks up trash when she walks to school.
5 She has a social media page.
6 She loves the superhero cartoon about her.
7 She wants three people to pick up trash every day.

7 **Work in pairs. Answer the questions.**

1 Which campaign would you choose to help? Why?
2 Felix and Nadia think that young people need to act to save the environment. What are arguments for and against this?

First conditional

1 Read the examples in the table. Choose the correct option to complete the rules.

Action	Result
If we **cut down** our trees,	we **won't have** clean air.
If we **wait** for adults to act,	it**'ll be** too late.
If we **don't recycle** plastic,	it**'ll go** into the oceans.

1 We use the first conditional to talk about **possible/certain** actions and their results.

2 After *if* we use **the simple present/*will* + base form**.

3 To talk about the result, we use **the simple present/*will* + base form.**

Order of clauses in conditional sentences

We can change the order of the clauses. When the *if* clause comes second, we don't use a comma.
We won't have clean air if we cut down trees.

2 Circle the correct option.

1 The streets **are/will be** cleaner if we **pick up/ will pick up** trash.

2 We **don't have/won't have** enough trees if we **cut/will cut** them down.

3 We **produce/will produce** less waste if we **recycle/will recycle** paper at school.

4 If we **plant/will plant** vegetables, we **don't need/won't need** to buy them.

5 If we all **do/will do** something, it **makes/ will make** a big difference.

3 Write sentences using the first conditional.

1 if / it / be sunny tomorrow / we / go to the park

2 you / be tired tomorrow / if / you / go to bed late

3 you / not pass your exams / if / you / not / study

4 if / the bus / not come soon / we / be late for class

5 I / call you / this evening / if / I / have time

Zero conditional

4 Read the examples in the table. Answer the questions.

Action	Result
If ocean animals **eat** plastic,	they **die**.
If we **cut down** trees,	animals **lose** their homes.

1 Is the result certain or possible?

2 What tense do we use to describe the action?

3 What tense do we use to describe the result?

5 Match 1–5 to a–e to make sentences. Write the verbs in the correct form.

1 If you ________ **(freeze)** water,

2 You ________ **(save)** electricity if

3 If it ________ **(not rain)** for a long time,

4 If you ________ **(not eat)**,

5 If you ________ **(put)** sugar in a drink,

a you ________ **(close)** the fridge door.

b it ________ **(taste)** sweet.

c plants ________ **(not grow)**.

d it ________ **(change)** to ice.

e you ________ **(feel)** hungry.

6 Complete the sentences so they are true for you. Use the first or zero conditional.

1 If it rains next weekend, ...

2 I'll be happy if ...

3 Our teacher gets annoyed if ...

4 If I get any money for my next birthday, ...

5 I usually stay in bed if ...

7 Circle the correct option.

GRAMMAR ROUND-UP

1 2 3 4 5 6 7 8

The family living plastic-free

Can you imagine living without plastic? It's **1 easier/easiest** than you think. That's the opinion of Rachel Benefield from New Zealand. If you go to her house, you **2 aren't seeing/ won't see** any plastic. She and her family stopped using it in 2017.

Rachel **3 listened/was listening** to a talk about waste in the oceans when she **4 was deciding/decided** to give up plastic. Now she only uses natural materials. She doesn't buy **5 many/much** food in supermarkets. She takes bottles and bags from home and goes to local stores instead. If food **6 comes/will come** from local stores, it's fresher, and it isn't **7 as/more** expensive as in supermarkets, she says.

Her family **8 usually/used** to throw away a lot of waste a week. Now they produce much less. They're just one family, but they are **9 help/ helping** to save the planet.

Reinforcement and Challenge Grammar bootcamp p124

Making decisions

1 Work in pairs. Read the invitation. What things do you need to buy if you have a party?

2 Watch the video. What do Rosie and Louis decide to buy?

3 Watch again. Which Key phrases do you hear?

4 Complete the dialogue with the Key phrases. Watch again and check.

Rosie So, what do we need to get ready for the party?

Louis Not much. Mum's getting the food and drinks.

Rosie 1 ________________ plates?

Louis We've got a lot at home, and glasses too. And it's better not to use plastic cups or plates anyway.

Rosie 2 ________________ . And no plastic straws either. They're terrible for the environment!

Louis But we need some decorations.

Rosie What do you 3 ________________ making our own? It'll be more fun if we make them.

Louis 4 ________________ the party's on Saturday. I don't think we'll have time.

Rosie You're 5 ________________ . 6 ________________ we can get some at the party shop?

Louis Why don't we go and see?

Rosie OK, 7 ________________ ! Let's go!

5 Create your own dialogue. Follow the steps in the Skills boost.

SKILLS BOOST

THINK
Choose one of the options:
a a barbecue **b** a picnic
Make a list of things that you need.
Try to make your picnic or barbecue 'green'!

PREPARE
Prepare a dialogue.

PRACTICE
Practice your dialogue. Take turns playing the different parts.

PERFORM
Act out your dialogue for the class.

6 Peer review **Listen to your classmates.**
1 How do they prepare for their barbecue/picnic?
2 Is it a 'green' barbecue/picnic? Why/Why not?
3 Which Key phrases do they use?

Key phrases

Discussing ideas: Do you think (that) … ?
What do you think about (+ noun or verb -*ing*)?
What about … ?
The good thing is that …

Agreeing and disagreeing: (That's a) good point.
Yes, but …
I'm not sure …
I agree. / You're right.
OK, good idea.

UK → US
Mum (UK) → Mom (US)
party shop (UK) → party store (US)

The Shower Timer - for shorter showers!

We use a lot of water in our homes. We use it to do things like wash clothes and take showers. Now, if you use the SHOWER TIMER, you'll save water every day!

What it does

The Shower Timer controls the time that you spend in the shower. It makes it easy for you to take a shorter shower, and so to save water.

How it works

You choose the time that you want to spend in the shower, for example two, three or five minutes. After that time, the water slowly turns off. An alarm rings to tell you that it's time to end your shower. Then the water stops.

Why use the Shower Timer?

- special features, such as a flexible timer
- easy to use
- saves water, electricity and money
- good for the environment

Save water, save the planet!

Do your part for the environment and cut your bills.

BUY THE SHOWER TIMER TODAY!

An advertisement

1 Work in pairs. Look at photos 1–4. What do you think each thing is?

2 Read the advertisement. Match the product with one of the pictures in exercise 1.

3 Read the advertisement again. Make notes.

Name of the product	*The Shower Timer*
Why people need it	
What it does	
How it works	
Why it's special	

4 Which of the following can you see in the advertisement?

- A short, interesting title
- A picture
- An important phrase about the product
- Headings
- Short phrases or expressions
- One long paragraph
- A summary – why people need this product

▶ Subskill: Giving examples

We use *for example*, *such as* and *like* when we give examples.

5 Find three sentences with the words ***for example***, ***such as*** and ***like*** in the advertisement.

6 Complete the sentences with ***for example***, ***such as*** or ***like*** and your own ideas.

1 You can use this in different rooms *like the living room and kitchen.*

2 You can use it with technology ______

3 You can recycle clothes ______

4 You can buy 'green' products for school ______

5 You can reuse a plastic bottle to make things ______

7 Write an advertisement for a 'green' product. Follow the steps in the Skills boost.

SKILLS BOOST

THINK

1 Think of a product. You can use one of the products in exercise 1 or invent one.

2 Make notes.

Name of the product	
Why people need it	
What it does	
How it works	
Why it's special	

PREPARE

- Draw a picture of your product or use a photo.
- Think of a title.
- Organize your notes in short paragraphs. Use headings.
- Think of an important phrase and a summary.
- Include two or three sentences for your advertisement with *for example*, *such as* or *like*.

____

____

____

____

____

____

____

____

____

WRITE

Write your advertisement.

CHECK

Read your advertisement and answer the questions.

1 Do you explain how the product will help if you buy it? ☐

2 Do you use *for example*, *such as* or *like*? ☐

3 Do you use the features in exercise 4? ☐

8 Peer review **Exchange your advertisement with other students. Which product do you think is most useful?**

Quick review

Grammar

will/won't + base form

We use *will/won't* + base form to talk about future predictions.

*We'**ll live** in 3D houses in the future.*

*It **won't take** a long time to build these houses.*

***Will** they **be** different from houses now?*

*Yes, they **will**. / No, they **won't**.*

We use *definitely*, *probably*, *possibly* and *definitely not* to say how certain we are that something will happen.

*They'**ll probably build** these houses in my country.*

*We **probably won't live** on the moon.*

We also use *might* + base form to say that something is possible in the future.

*We **might** design our own houses in the future.*

*I **might** move to another country.*

First conditional

We use the first conditional to talk about possible actions in the present or future, and their results.

To make the first conditional, use *if* + present, *will/won't* + base form.

*If we all **pick up** trash, our streets **will be** cleaner.*

*If we **don't plant** trees, we **won't have** clean air.*

We can change the order of the two parts of the sentence.

If the 'if' part comes first, use a comma. If it's second, don't use a comma.

***If I pass** the test, **I'll be** happy.*

***I'll be** happy **if I pass** the test.*

Zero conditional

We use the zero conditional to talk about facts, or things that are always true.

To make the zero conditional, use *if/when* + simple present, simple present.

***When** you **freeze** water, it **changes** to ice.*

***If** I **don't get** enough sleep, I **feel** tired.*

Vocabulary

26 Rooms

bathroom, bedroom, garage, hall, kitchen, living room, office, stairs, yard

27 Furniture

armchair, basin, bookshelf, carpet, closet, couch, cupboard, curtains, fridge, oven, sink, trash can, washing machine

28 Your environment

nouns: pollution, recycling bins, trash, waste

verbs: plant (a tree), recycle, reduce, reuse

phrasal verbs: cut down, give up, pick up, throw away, turn down, turn off, turn on, turn up

5 Project

WDYT?
(What do you think?)

How can we improve our environment?

TASK: Conduct a green audit of your school and make proposals for change.

Learning outcomes

1 I can conduct an audit and make a proposal about how to make our school greener.

2 I can solve different types of problems.

3 I can use appropriate language from the unit.

Graphic organizer → Project planner p132

1 Watch the video of students presenting their proposal. What aspect of school life do they talk about?

STEP 1: THINK

2 Work in groups of three. Answer the questions about the poster in the Model project.

1 Is the information well organized and clear?
2 Are there any pictures or photos?
3 Do they include survey results?
4 Do they say how they got the information?
5 Do they give a variety of suggestions?

STEP 2: PLAN

3 Work in your groups. Choose one aspect of your school environment you can improve. Use an idea from the box or your own.

food waste | green spaces | plants and nature | use of electricity | use of paper | use of water

4 Plan your audit. You can get information by ...

- preparing survey questions to find out what people do or their opinions (other students, teachers)
- preparing interview questions to ask people who are responsible (teachers, principal, other people who work in the school)
- observing and counting

5 Do your audit. Note all the answers and information carefully.

STEP 3: CREATE

6 Work in groups. Read the tips in the Super skills box and practice saying the Key phrases with your group.

CRITICAL THINKING — SUPER SKILLS

Solving different types of problems

Tips

Find a solution which works for each type of problem (content, presentation, ...).

Discuss before you write.

Write a plan in pencil before you start.

Key phrases

OK, so how are we going to organize the space?

We could put (...) here.

Are we going to include (headings, pictures, ...)?

People say (...) so we could suggest (...).

I think (...) would be a good idea.

7 Work together to create your poster. Read the checklist in exercise 2 to help you. Use the tips and Key phrases in the Super skills box.

Model project

Recycling at Cranbourne High School

GREEN AUDIT

Number of trash cans: **78**

Classrooms 24
Playground 8
Other rooms 12
Halls and general 12
Cafeteria 12
Kitchens 10

Places where you can separate waste: **9** (paper / plastic)

Classrooms 7
Art room 1
Cafeteria 1

Students who separate waste in our class: **43%**

Waste collection:

General waste – every day
Paper recycling – once a week
Plastics – once a week
Glass – twice a month

People responsible: Mr. Mackey (head of kitchen), Mrs. Grove (head of cleaning team)

How we conducted our audit: counting, observation, interviews

PROPOSAL

Have recycling bins in every classroom
Students take turns taking recycling to central recycling points
Stop selling water in plastic bottles at the school store
Organize a recycling awareness week: Visits to the recycling center
Effort to reduce waste by 50%
Talk by council recycling officer

STEP 4: PRESENT

8 **Read the *How to* ... tips on p132. Then prepare to present your poster to other students.**

9 Peer review **Present your poster to another group. As you listen to your classmates, think about the questions.**

1 Does the information surprise you?
2 Which proposal can make the most difference?
3 What do your classmates do well when they present their poster?

5 FINAL REFLECTION

1 The task
Is the poster clear and attractive?
Is the audit information and the section on proposals clear?

2 Super skill
Did you solve different types of problems? Give examples.

3 Language
In your poster and presentation, did you use language from the unit? Give examples.

6 Experience

WDYT?
(What do you think?)

Why might it be a good idea to try new things?

Vocabulary: collocations: experiences; music

Grammar: present perfect for experience; *ever* and *never*

Reading: a profile about a young tech entrepreneur

Listening: a conversation about finding a present

Speaking: talking about experience

Writing: an e-postcard

Project: make memes of things for classmates to do before they're 18

Video skills p73

Real-world speaking p79

Project pp82–83

Give it a try!

1 ____________

2 ____________

3 ____________

4 ____________

5 ____________

6 ____________

7 ____________

8 ____________

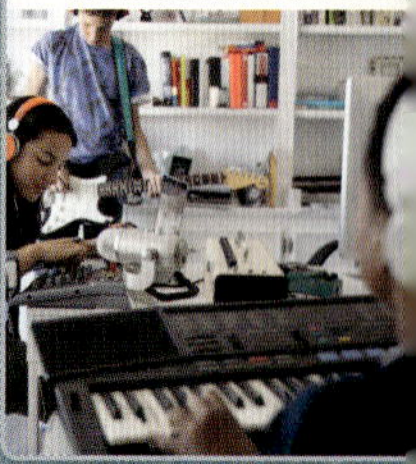

Collocations: experiences

1 Match the verbs in the box with nouns a–h to form collocations.

be eat go meet play stay visit write

a ________ a theme park

b ________ a blog

c ________ a famous person

d ________ sushi

e ________ on TV

f ________ to a concert

g ________ at a youth hostel

h ________ baseball

2 Complete the sentences with the verbs in exercise 1.

1 Which famous person would you like to ________ ? Why?

2 Do you ever ________ at youth hostels? When?

3 Is it common for people in your country to ________ sushi?

4 How often do you ________ to concerts?

5 Would you like to ________ on TV? Why?

6 Which theme park would you most like to ________ ?

7 Does anyone you know ________ a blog?

9 ________________

10 ________________

11 ________________

12 ________________

13 ________________

14 ________________

15 ________________

16 ________________

3 **Work in pairs. Ask and answer the questions in exercise 2.**

Learning phrases

It's easier to make your own sentences when you learn the meaning of phrases, not just words.

4 **Write the phrases in the box next to photos 1–16.**

act in a play | bake a cake | build a sandcastle | do a bungee jump | fly a kite | go zip lining | keep a diary | make a snowman | play laser tag | record music | ride a horse | sing karaoke | sleep under the stars | swim with dolphins | take a dance class | travel to another continent

5 **Choose three experiences from exercise 4 for a person who likes:**

- adventure
- music, theater and dance
- outdoor activities
- doing things at home

6 **Complete the sentences with a collocation in exercise 4. Make necessary changes.**

1 I hate the idea of jumping off a bridge. I would never ________________ !
2 I often ________________ for my mom's birthday.
3 I'd like to ________________ one day. People say they're the friendliest ocean animals.
4 My brother ________________ . He doesn't let anyone read it.
5 I don't mind going to the theater, but I wouldn't like to ________________ .
6 I used to ________________ every day when we went to the beach on vacation.
7 We go camping once a year and ________________ .

7 **Work in pairs. Answer the questions about the experiences in exercise 4.**

1 Which would you like to do? Why?
2 Which would you never do? Why not?

CELEBRITY CORNER

Nicole Kidman has a license for an extreme sport. Which one?

VIDEO SKILLS

8 **Watch the video. What things have Chloe and John done?**

9 **Work in pairs. Discuss the questions.**

1 What is the main reason for this video?
  a to give information
  b to entertain
  c to make you think
2 How does the video get and hold your attention? Think about the photos, the vloggers' voices, body language and where they look.

A profile

1 Work in pairs. How many verb and noun phrases can you make in one minute?

act bake do meet record see sing start take write

a bungee jump a cake a company a dance class a famous person a musical a news story in a play karaoke music

2 29 Read and listen to the article. Which activities in exercise 1 …

1 does/did Jenk do?
2 can you read about on his website?

3 Read the article again. Which three sentences are true?

1 The website is only for teenagers.
2 It has stories about things that are interesting for teens.
3 When he was younger, Jenk went to sports games every weekend.
4 His friends at school wanted to go with him to fun events.
5 His mother gave information to his friends about things to do and see.
6 Jenk doesn't have time to think of ideas because he has a lot of hobbies.

4 Read the article again. Correct the false sentences in exercise 3.

Subskill: Answering questions in your own words

When you answer questions, find the information in the text. Then think of another way to say the same thing. *He is a tech entrepreneur.* → *He started a company using technology.*

5 Read the article again. Answer the questions in your own words.

1 What information can you find on the website?
2 Where was Jenk when he first had the idea for the site?
3 What did Jenk do at school before he started the site?
4 What types of activities does Jenk like?
5 What is Jenk's main job on the website?
6 What plans does Jenk have for the site?

6 Word work Match the definitions to the words in bold in the text.

1 finding new facts or information ________
2 visits to a website ________
3 concentrates on, pays attention to ________
4 reach the whole world ________
5 organized activities, such as sports competitions ________
6 sports or activities that are exciting and dangerous ________

7 Complete the sentences with the words in exercise 6.

1 Most people play football or basketball, but ________ are becoming popular.
2 A video on YouTube can get millions of ________ a day.
3 The concert is one of the most important ________ of the year.
4 With online shopping, it's easy for small companies to ________ .
5 We did a lot of ________ for our history project.
6 Our technology course ________ computer programming.

CRITICAL THINKING SUPER SKILLS

1 **Remember** What different types of information can you find at iCoolKid.com? Which do you think are most interesting?

2 **Evaluate** Why do you think the website is successful?

3 **Create** Imagine you want to make a website about things that are cool where you live.

- Choose three ideas in different categories (music etc.)
- Tell the class about one of your ideas.

Meet Jenk, the founder of iCoolKid

Jenk Oz is a tech entrepreneur. He's met a lot of celebrities, including Adele. He's appeared in documentaries and music videos, and he's acted in a play in a London theater.
The amazing thing is, he's still a teenager!

Jenk's company, a digital platform called iCoolKid, is a guide to all things cool to see and do. It's designed for eight- to 15-year-olds, and **focuses on** pop culture, tech and **events**. It has stories on everything from baking a cake with a 3D printer to doing a bungee jump on skis. You can even sing karaoke there. Jenk describes it as a place for young people to hang out and never get bored.

'It's a place where young people can hang out and never get bored.'

The idea for the site came to Jenk when he was eight. Every Monday morning, his teacher asked about their weekend. He realized that he always did different things from his classmates. They sometimes saw a soccer or rugby game, but he went to musicals or other different events. His friends started to ask, 'Can I come with you?' Jenk's mother decided to send them an email every week with ideas about what to do. Jenk presented the email as a school project, and the website grew from there.

Jenk's own hobbies are a big part of his **research**. In his free time, he records music and takes dance classes. He sings and plays four musical instruments well. He loves **extreme sports**; he's been go-karting and sky-diving. He's a big fan of fashion too.

Jenk hasn't written all the stories on his site. He has a team who helps him, but he decides what's cool. And he has big plans for the future. iCoolKid has between 1,000 and 2,000 **hits** a day, and he wants to increase that to a million. He also plans to **go global** and write articles for people around the world.

Present perfect: affirmative and negative

1 **Read the sentences in the table. Answer the questions.**

Subject	*have*	Past participle
I/you/we/they	have	**met** a lot of celebrities.
	haven't	**acted** in a West End play.
he/she/it	has	**taken** dance classes.
	hasn't	**written** all the stories.

1 Are the sentences about the past or now?
2 Do we know exactly when these things happened?
3 How do we make the present perfect in the affirmative? How do we make it in the negative?
4 Which past participle in the table is regular? How do we make the past participle of regular verbs?

2 **Complete the sentences with the affirmative or negative of *have* and regular past participles.**

1 She ________________ **(visit)** cities all over the world.
2 I ________________ **(not try)** zip lining.
3 They ________________ **(play)** baseball.
4 He ________________ **(not stay)** in a big hotel.
5 We ________________ **(travel)** overseas.

3 **Look at the irregular verbs on pp134-135. Write the past participles of these irregular verbs.**

be do eat fly give have make meet
see sing sleep swim take write

be – been *do – done*

4 **Write the sentences in the present perfect.**

1 I / not eat / Thai food
2 My friends / swim / in the ocean
3 My cousin / not take / any dance classes
4 We / not write / a book
5 My aunt / do / a bungee jump
6 I / not meet / anyone famous

been* and *gone

Go has two past participles, *been* and *gone*.
Donna has gone to a concert. (She's there now.)
I've been to Scotland twice. (I'm not there now.)

5 **Write two sentences that are true for you and two that are false. Use the words in the box.**

fly a kite go to a live concert play laser tag
travel by plane try zip lining write a song

6 **Work in pairs. Guess which of your partner's sentences from exercise 5 are true and which are false.**

7 **Complete the article with the present perfect of the verbs in the box.**

do eat go not drink not spend
not try swim take

Famous adventurers

You'd be surprised how many famous people like doing unusual things. Both Katy Perry and Justin Bieber **1** ________________ a bungee jump in New Zealand. Taylor Swift **2** ________________ a selfie with a kangaroo, and Rihanna **3** ________________ with sharks. Orlando Bloom **4** ________________ all his time making movies, he **5** ________________ to Antarctica and tried snowboarding there too! Salma Hayek **6** ________________ all kinds of insects – , she loves them! (I know they're on the menu in some countries, but I **7** ________________ them!)

8 **Answer the question to solve the Brain teaser.**

BRAIN TEASER

Annie, Hugo, Ari and Maya live in New York. They have each visited one city – Tokyo, London, Los Angeles or Paris. Read the clues.

Annie hasn't been to Japan.

Hugo has traveled to Europe.

Ari has never visited a different country.

Annie has seen the Eiffel Tower.

Maya has tried sushi where it's a typical dish.

Which cities have they each visited?

Music

1 Look at the information. Answer the questions.

1 What type of present can we see?
2 Would you like to receive this present?
3 What are the advantages and disadvantages of this type of present?

Looking for the perfect gift for the **musician** in your life? It doesn't matter what style they prefer: **classical music**, **pop**, **hip hop** or **jazz** – our music experiences have something for everybody.

2 Look at the words in bold in exercise 1 and find ...

1 four styles of music
2 three people
3 two instruments
4 one group of musicians

3 Add the words in the box to the correct category in exercise 2. Do you know any more words for each group?

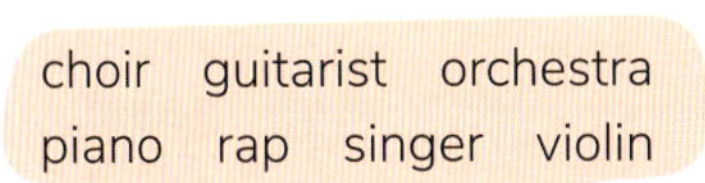

choir guitarist orchestra piano rap singer violin

4 30 Listen to some sounds and describe what you can hear. Use the vocabulary in exercises 1 and 3.

A conversation

5 31 Listen to a conversation between two people and answer the questions.

1 What is the boy's problem? ____________
2 What is the girl's solution? ____________

Subskill: Noticing differences between the question and what you hear

Before you listen, look at the question and think of different ways in which the information might be given. For example, to answer *What does Zack's father like?*, you might hear *He likes ... He's into ... He's interested in ...*

6 Listen again. Complete the table.

Zack's father likes		Possible presents for Zack's father	
sports	*no*	DJ experience	
clothes		masterclass with expert	
music		recording studio session	

7 Listen again and find eight mistakes in this summary of the dialogue.

Zack and Lily are discussing birthday presents for Zack's cousin. He's going to be 40 next month. Zack has given experience boxes before; they are big boxes with a present inside. Zack and Lily look at a website called Experience Music Now. One option is to record your own song in a studio with a professional singer. Another is to visit a professional musician and write a song together. Zack decides to buy this gift.

8 Work in pairs. Correct the mistakes from exercise 7.

*They are discussing presents for Zack's **father**.*

9 Work in pairs. Discuss the questions.

1 Can you play an instrument?
2 If not, what would you like to do/play?

Pronunciation: Consonant clusters p129

Present perfect: questions

1 **Complete the tables with the examples in the box.**

> **Have** you ever **given** him an experience box?
> No, I **haven't**.
> **Has** he ever **been** to a recording studio?
> No, never.

Questions				
1 ______	I, you, we, they	2 ______	**seen**	a pop star?
Has	he, she, it			

Short answers		
Yes,	3 ______ , you, we, they	**have.**
	he, she, it	**has.**
No,	I, you, we, they	4 ______
	he, she, it	**hasn't.**
	5 ______	

2 **Match questions 1–4 to answers a–d.**

1 Have you ever been skiing?
2 Have you read this book?
3 Has your mother ever been to the United States?
4 Have we done this exercise before?
a No, but she's been to Canada.
b Yes, I've read it twice.
c Yes, we go to the Alps every year.
d No, I don't think we have.

ever and *never*

> *Ever* means 'at any time in your life'. We use *ever* in questions.
> *Never* means 'at no time in your life'. We use *never* with an affirmative verb to give a negative idea.
> *Have you **ever** been to Buenos Aires?*
> *No, I've **never** been to Argentina.*

3 **Make sentences with *ever* and *never*.**

1 you / break your leg (?)
Have you ever broken your leg?
2 he / play golf (–)
3 you visit / the royal palace (?)
4 I / play Monopoly (–)
5 she / travel / by plane (?)
6 he / have / a job (–)
7 we / study / Latin (–)
8 you / be on a motorcycle (?)

4 **Match words from each box to make a question.**

Have you ever bought tickets for a concert?

~~buy~~	a famous musician
download	live music
give	money to a street musician
meet	music from the Internet
play	the drums
see	~~tickets for a concert~~

5 **Work in pairs. Ask and answer the questions in exercise 4.**

6 **Circle the correct option.**

GRAMMAR ROUND-UP

1 2 3 4 5 6 7 8

Renata Flores is a singer from Ayacucho in Peru. She became a big hit when nearly two million people watched her version of the Michael Jackson song 'The Way You Make Me Feel' on YouTube. **1** (…) so special about the song? Renata sang it in Quechua.

Quechua is Peru's second language. Ten percent of the 30 million population **2** (…) Quechua and another 4.5 million people speak it in Ecuador, Bolivia, Argentina, Colombia and Brazil. But the language was unpopular for many years. Students **3** (…) Quechua in school and **4** (…) parents didn't want their children to learn the language. And if **5** (…) a language, it disappears.

Renata herself couldn't **6** (…) Quechua well, so her grandmother helped her translate the song from English. Renata is now a celebrity in Peru and she **7** (…) on a project to make young people proud to speak Quechua. She continues to post on YouTube and she **8** (…) songs by people like Bob Marley and Alicia Keys.

1 a What was b What did
2 a speak b are speaking
3 a didn't used to learn b didn't use to learn
4 a a lots of b a lot of
5 a nobody will speak b nobody speaks
6 a speak b to speak
7 a is worked b has worked
8 a has recorded b have recorded

Reinforcement and Challenge Grammar bootcamp p125

Talking about experience

1 Work in pairs. Look at the ad. What abilities and experience are important for the job?

2 Watch the video. Do they decide Diego can help with the musical? Why/Why not?

3 Watch again. Which Key phrases do you hear?

4 Complete the dialogue with the Key phrases. Watch again and check.

Flynn Diego? Hi, I'm Flynn.

Diego Hi, nice to meet you.

Flynn So, why do you **1** ______ to help with the musical?

Diego Well, I like the theater, so it sounds like a cool thing to do.

Flynn Have you **2** ______ done this type of work before?

Diego Not **3** ______ , not with a musical.

Flynn And do you have any **4** ______ with sound or lighting?

Diego My brother's a DJ, so I know a little **5** ______ sound.

Flynn Oh yeah? **6** ______ you use a mixing desk and all the equipment?

Diego Yeah, I can.

Flynn OK, that sounds good. Are you free to meet Wednesdays and Fridays after school?

Diego Sure, no problem.

Flynn OK, cool. So, see you Wednesday in the school auditorium.

Diego Great.

5 Create your own dialogue. Follow the steps in the Skills boost.

SKILLS BOOST

THINK
Think of an event at your school when they need volunteers (e.g. a school concert, disco, party, open day ...). Decide what abilities and experience are important for the volunteers.

PREPARE
Prepare a dialogue. Remember to include interview questions from the Key phrases box.
Why are you interested in ... ? Have you ever ... ?

PRACTICE
Practice your dialogue.

PERFORM
Act out your dialogue for the class.

6 **Peer review** Listen to your classmates and answer the questions.

1 What abilities and experience did the candidate have?
2 Do you think they got the job? Why/Why not?

Key phrases

General interview questions:
Why do you want to (help with the musical)?
Why are you interested (in this)?

Questions about experience/abilities:
Have you ever done (this type of work) before?
Do you have any experience of (doing lighting)?
Can you (use a mixing desk)?

Talking about your experience/abilities:
I can (read music).
I know a little about (sound).
I don't know anything about (musicals).
(Can you ... ?) Not really.

US → UK

I like the **theater**. (US) → I like the **theatre**. (UK)
See you **Wednesday**. (US) → See you **on Wednesday**. (UK)

Dear Leah,

I'm having a great time here in Indiana. It's a camp where you can do lots of outdoor activities. We've ridden horses and slept under the stars. Yesterday we went zip lining, which was amazing. You should give it a try!

The people are really nice too. I'm sharing a room with three guys from Boston who are really fun.

We're staying in a youth hostel which is in the mountains. It's near a lake where you can swim and canoe. It's so beautiful – you should come with me next year.

OK, well that's all my news for now. I hope you're having a good summer – see you on the 21st.

Alex

PS I almost forgot: I met a boy who knows you – Danny Zhao – he said to say Hi.

80 Lansdowne Road
Portsmouth, NH
03801

Dear Leah,

I'm having a great time here in Indiana. It's a camp where you can do lots of outdoor activities. We've ridden horses and slept under the stars. Yesterday we went zip lining, which was amazing. You should give it a try!

The people are really nice too. I'm sharing a room with three guys from Boston who are really fun.

We're staying in a youth hostel which is in the mountains. It's near a lake where you can swim and canoe. It's so beautiful – you should come with me next year.

OK, well that's all my news for now. I hope you're having a good summer – see you on the 21st.

Alex

PS I almost forgot: I met a boy who knows you – Danny Zhao – he said to say Hi.

An e-postcard

1 **Work in pairs. Look at the postcards and discuss the similarities and differences.**

2 **Read the message on the e-postcard. Why is Alex writing?**

3 **Read the message again. What information does Alex include?**

1 the activities he's doing
2 the weather
3 the other people
4 the food
5 where he is staying
6 someone Leah knows
7 two suggestions

4 **Read again and answer the questions.**

1 How do you say 'Hello' in a letter or postcard?
2 What's the first thing you often write about?
3 What type of information is in each paragraph?
4 How do you finish a postcard?
5 What is a 'PS'?

Subskill: *who*, *where* and *which*

We use *who*, *where* and *which* to connect two sentences.

I'm sharing a room with three guys from Boston. The guys are really fun. → I'm sharing a room with three guys from Boston who are really fun.

5 **Find more examples of sentences with *who*, *where* and *which*. Then complete the rules.**

1 Use ______ to connect sentences about people.
2 Use ______ to connect sentences about places.
3 Use ______ to connect sentences about things.

6 **Complete the sentences with *who*, *where* or *which*.**

1 I have a friend ______ has swum with dolphins.
2 We visited a park ______ you can play laser tag.
3 Have you ever met someone ______ can speak four languages?
4 A kite is a type of toy ______ flies.
5 A supermarket is a store ______ you can buy food and other things.

7 **Write a postcard to a friend. Follow the steps in the Skills boost.**

SKILLS BOOST

THINK

1 In pairs, think of a new place or experience you could write about on a postcard.

2 Make notes about some of the following:

- where you're staying ______
- the food ______
- the weather ______
- the activities you're doing ______
______
- the other people ______
______

PREPARE

1 Organize your notes into paragraphs and decide on the best order.

______
______
______
______
______
______
______
______
______
______
______

2 Write some sentences connected with *who*, *where* or *which*.

______
______
______

WRITE

Write your postcard individually. Use the example and exercise 4 to help you.

CHECK

Read your postcard and answer the questions.

1 Do you use the present perfect to talk about experiences? ☐

2 Do you use *who*, *where* and *which* to connect sentences? ☐

3 Do you organize the information clearly? ☐

8 Peer review **Exchange your postcard with another student. Would you like to visit this place/do these activities? Say why/why not.**

Quick review

Grammar

Present perfect

Affirmative and negative

We use the present perfect to talk about experiences in the past, often without saying exactly when we did things.

*She**'s traveled** all over the world.*

Make the affirmative with *have/has* + past participle.

Make the negative with *haven't/hasn't* + past participle.

***I've eaten** octopus, but I **haven't tried** sushi.*

Past participles

Some past participles are regular. We add *-ed* (like the simple past).

*repeat → repeat**ed***   *open → open**ed***

Some past participles are irregular.

be → been   *do → done*   *see → seen*   *speak → spoken*

(For a list of irregular verbs, see pp134–135.)

been and *gone*

We use *been* when a person went somewhere and has returned.

We use *gone* when a person went somewhere and is still there.

*I've **been** to France three times.*

*We don't have P.E. today because Mr. Shaw has **gone** home.*

Questions

We form questions with *have* + subject + past participle.

We often use *ever* in questions. It means 'at any time in your life'.

***Have** you **ever been** camping? No, I haven't.*

We can use *Wh-* questions like *How many times* with the present perfect.

*How many times **have** you **seen** this movie?*

Vocabulary

32 Collocations: experiences

act in a play, bake a cake, be on TV, build a sandcastle, do a bungee jump, eat sushi, fly a kite, go to a concert, go zip lining, keep a diary, make a snowman, meet a famous person, play baseball, play laser tag, record music, ride a horse, sing karaoke, sleep under the stars, stay at a youth hostel, swim with dolphins, take a dance class, travel to another continent, visit a theme park, write a blog

33 Music

band, choir, classical, composer, DJ, drum, guitarist, hip hop, jazz, keyboard, musician, piano, pop, orchestra, rap, singer, violin

6 Project

WDYT?
(What do you think?)

Why might it be a good idea to try new things?

TASK: Make memes of things for classmates to do before they're 18.

Learning outcomes

1 I can find out about other students' experiences and make a list of goals.

2 I can collaborate with a partner.

3 I can use appropriate language from the unit.

Graphic organizer → Project planner p132

1 Watch a video of students presenting their memes. What experiences do they suggest?

STEP 1: THINK

2 Read the questionnaire in the Model project. What does it ask about?

adventure dance fears food
hobbies music people travel

3 Add two more ideas to the list of topics in exercise 2.

STEP 2: PLAN

4 Work in pairs. Write a questionnaire with ten questions to ask your classmates about their experiences. Use ideas from exercise 2.

1 Have you ever ...

5 Work with another pair. Take turns asking your questions.

6 Make a table with things that your classmates have done, and things that they haven't done.

Things they've done	Things they haven't done
been to a live concert	*tried Korean food*

STEP 3: CREATE

7 Work in pairs. Read the tips in the Super skills box and practice saying the Key phrases with your partner.

COLLABORATION — SUPER SKILLS

Working together to achieve your goals

Tips

Take turns speaking and listening.

Make sure you agree with decisions.

Share the work equally.

Key phrases

I think we should include ...

I'm not clear about this.

Let's talk about this more before we decide.

OK, do we both agree?

I wrote last time, so I think it's your turn now.

Can I give you a hand?

You did that last time, so I'll do it this time.

8 Look at the table in exercise 6. Make a list of eight things to do for the classmates that you interviewed. Use the tips and Key phrases in the Super skills box.

9 Read the *How to ...* tips on p132. Then work together to create eight memes.

Model project

1 Have you traveled to many countries?
2 What types of food from other countries have you tried?
3 Can you dance? Have you ever taken a dance class?
4 Do you like music? Have you ever been to a live concert?
5 Have you ever met a person from another country?
6 What are you afraid of?

STEP 4: PRESENT

10 **Present your memes to the pair you interviewed.**

11 Peer review **Listen to your classmates and answer the questions.**

1 Do you agree with the list that your classmates prepared for you? Why/Why not?
2 Are the memes attractive and interesting?

6 FINAL REFLECTION

1 The task

Did you include a variety of questions in your questionnaire? Give examples.

Did you choose appropriate experiences? Give reasons.

2 Super skill

Did you work together to achieve your goals? Give examples.

3 Language

Did you use the language from the unit? Give examples.

7 My stuff

What does your bedroom say about you?

WDYT? (What do you think?)

How important are personal possessions?

Vocabulary: describing things; adjective suffixes

Grammar: present perfect with *for* and *since*; present perfect and simple past; time expressions

Reading: a feature article about collecting

Listening: an interview with a teenage minimalist

Speaking: asking about lost and found objects

Writing: a personal email

Project: prepare a 'Me Box' and present the items in a video

Video skills p85

Real-world speaking p91

Project pp94–95

Photo A

Describing things

1 Work in pairs. Answer the questions.

1 Look at the photos. How many things can you name?

2 What does each room say about its owner?

2 Look at the photos again. Use the words in the box to describe what you see in the photos. There are more materials than you need.

cotton glass gold metal paper plastic silver wood wool

The shelves are made of wood.

3 Work in pairs. Say what objects 1–9 are usually made of.

1 a key
2 a door
3 a notebook
4 a shirt
5 a winner's medal
6 most water bottles
7 a mirror
8 a sweater
9 knives and forks

What's a key made of?

It's made of metal.

Let's start with your shelves.

- **Are they organized or messy?**
- **What do you have on them?**
- **Do you have photos? Who/what do they show?**

4 **Read the descriptions. Can you identify the things in the photos?**

Photo A

1 It's black and white and made of metal and **hard** plastic. I think it's the most **valuable** thing in the room.

2 This is **square** and about 30 cm across. It's **heavy**. You need it to hear number 1.

3 It's an unusual shape. It has thin metal legs, so it's probably quite **light**.

Photo B

4 There are two or three of them, all **medium-sized**. One is **plain**, but the other one is **patterned** with small pink spots. The red one looks really **soft**.

5 It's **round** and it's really **tiny** – about the size of a large orange. It's silly when the world is so **huge** – I don't know how you can actually see the countries!

5 **Write the words in bold in exercise 4 under the correct heading. Can you add any more?**

How things feel
How much they cost
The shape
The design
How big things are

6 **Complete the facts about diamonds using adjectives from exercise 5.**

Everyone knows that diamonds are the world's most **1** ________ stones and cost thousands of dollars.

Eighty percent of diamonds are **2** ________ and too small to use, but some are **3** ________ : the Cullinan Diamond weighed over 600 grams!

A 'brilliant cut' diamond that looks **4** ________ actually has 58 different sides!

The diamond is so **5** ________ it's very useful for cutting other materials.

7 **Write descriptions of things in your classroom.**

Describing things

We say *it's made of* to describe the material.
When we talk about how big things are, we can say: *It's about the size of (an orange) / 15 cm across / this big* (and show the size with your hands).

VIDEO SKILLS

8 **Work in pairs. Watch the video and discuss the questions.**

1 What presents does the vlogger get?
2 Why is this type of video popular?
3 Do you like this type of video? Why/why not?

A feature article

1 **Work in pairs. Discuss the questions.**

1 Have you ever collected anything? If so, what?

2 Do you know anyone who collects anything interesting or unusual?

2 **Look at the three photos at the top of the page. How do they relate to the theme of collecting?**

3 34 **Read and listen to the article and answer the questions.**

1 What are the three collections in the article?

____

2 Why is each collection virtual?

____

4 **Read the text again. Which collection ... ?**

1 is a project between two big organizations

2 became very popular very quickly

3 is a new version of a traditional hobby

4 welcomes visitors from all over the world

5 can help you make a lot of money

5 **Read the text again. Are the statements true or false?**

1 More than six million people visit the *Museum of the World* every year.

2 All the objects in the *Museum of the World* are from ancient history.

3 With CryptoKitties®, you can be creative.

4 A single CryptoKitty sold for more than $100,000.

5 Doug Taron still catches butterflies.

6 Butterfly collecting now is more environmentally friendly.

6 **Correct the false sentences in exercise 5.**

▶ Subskill: Understanding unfamiliar words

If you see a word you don't know, keep reading before you check a dictionary. Use the context to help you understand the meaning.

7 Word work **Match the definitions to the words in bold in the text.**

1 a large area of land made of many countries ________

2 with the same meaning, importance, size, etc. as something else ________

3 unkind or causing pain to other people or animals ________

4 find and keep a person or animal ________

5 something that has a good result or is very popular ________

6 places people want to visit or see ________

8 **The words in bold are in the wrong sentence. Correct the sentences.**

1 The Eiffel Tower is the most popular **hit** in Paris.

____

2 One inch is the **continent** of 2.5 centimeters.

____

3 I'm a vegetarian. I think it's **catch** to eat animals.

____

4 Everyone loves that song. It's a big **attraction**.

____

5 I want to visit every **equivalent** in the world.

____

6 The police couldn't **cruel** the bank robbers.

____

CRITICAL THINKING — SUPER SKILLS

1 Remember What were the three reasons for having a virtual collection in the article?

2 Analyze Which do you think is the most important reason? Why?

3 Evaluate What qualities do you need to be a good collector? What do you think we can learn from collecting?

A NEW WAY TO COLLECT

Collecting has been a popular hobby for many years and people collect everything from comic books and coins to pencils and postcards. But now some people are collecting in a different way with a virtual collection. We find out why.

A MUSEUM ANYONE CAN VISIT

The British Museum is one of London's most popular **attractions** and nearly six million people visit it every year. But what if you can't get to London? No problem: with the *Museum of the World* project, the British Museum has worked with Google to create an amazing interactive experience. You can choose a **continent** or a moment in history and go back to see everything from Ancient Egyptian shoes to an Aztec knife. They have objects from 2 million BC right up to the present day. It's free and it doesn't matter where you live: this is a museum for everyone.

COLLECTING THINGS ON YOUR COMPUTER

In 2017, gaming fans quickly went crazy for a new type of game: CryptoKitties. In this game, people make virtual cats. They decide on the body, coloring and characteristics they want and then buy and sell them online. CryptoKitties has been a huge **hit**. Since 2017, players have spent the **equivalent** of around $30 million. One CryptoKitty sold for $140,000!

COLLECTING THINGS THAT YOU CAN'T TAKE WITH YOU

In the early part of the 20th century, when people collected butterflies, they used to **catch** them, kill them and then put them in a special box. Today, that sounds like a very **cruel** hobby. But that doesn't mean you can't collect butterflies. Doug Taron has had a butterfly collection since he was seven, but now he collects them virtually. He still finds butterflies in their habitat and keeps information about them; but now he collects photographs, not butterflies.

CELEBRITY CORNER

Some famous people have unusual collections. What does **Leonardo DiCaprio** collect?

Present perfect with *for* and *since*

1 Read the examples and circle the correct option to complete the rules.

Collecting has been a popular hobby **for** many years.

How long have you been interested in collecting stamps? **For** six months.

Doug Taron has had a butterfly collection **since** he was seven.

1. We use *for* and *since* with the **present perfect/ simple present** to answer the question 'How long?'
2. We use *for* and *since* when the action is **finished/unfinished**.
3. We use **for/since** to refer to the beginning of the time period.
4. We use **for/since** to refer to the duration of the time period.

2 Copy and complete the table with the words in the box.

2012 9 o'clock a long time April five years I was eight lunchtime many years ~~ten minutes~~ three weeks Tuesday we arrived

for	*since*
ten minutes	

3 Complete the sentences with *for* or *since*.

1. They've lived here ______ September.
2. I've had this phone ______ six months.
3. We've been at the school ______ 2018.
4. He hasn't seen his grandma ______ a long time.
5. She's had the same bike ______ the last two years.
6. I've been a fan of Disney movies ______ I was a child.
7. I haven't had anything to eat ______ breakfast.
8. Where have you been? I've been here ______ hours!

4 Rewrite the sentences with *for* or *since* so the meaning is the same.

1. I've had this jacket for three months. (It's May.)
   I've had this jacket since February.
2. Fatima's been sick since Tuesday. (It's Thursday.)
3. Jake's been on the football team since September. (It's January.)
4. We've lived in this house since 2018. (It's 2020.)
5. We've had exams for the last four days. (It's Friday.)
6. The weather has been great for a week. (It's May 27th.)

5 Complete the text with *for* and *since*.

Thirteen-year-old Lily Connors from Swansea, Wales, has been a huge fan of TV sci-fi series *Doctor Who*® **1** ______ she was a small child, and she and her family have watched it at her grandparents' house **2** ______ many years. Lily has also collected toys, cards and other *Doctor Who* objects **3** ______ nearly ten years and she has a very big collection. In fact, she has been the Guinness World Record® holder **4** ______ 2017. She's had three of the figures in her collection **5** ______ she was just four years old and she now has over 6,000 items. But Lily's not the only champion in the family. Her brother, Tom Connors, has been a record-holder in street basketball **6** ______ years and currently holds 16 world records.

6 Write questions with *How long*.

1. have / your phone
   How long have you had your phone?
2. be / at this school
3. know / your best friend
4. be / in this class
5. live / in this town
6. be / at school today

7 Work in pairs. Ask and answer the questions in exercise 6. Use *for* or *since*.

How long have had your phone?

For about three years, I think. How about you?

Since last year.

8 Answer the question to solve the Brain teaser.

BRAIN TEASER

Alfie has been at the bus stop for ten minutes longer than Jan, who has been at the bus stop for 15 minutes longer than Carl. Carl has been at the bus stop since 3:30 and it is now 3:40.

How long has Alfie been at the bus stop and what time did he arrive?

Reinforcement and Challenge Grammar bootcamp pp125–126

Pronunciation: *for*, *since* and sentence stress p129

Adjective suffixes

1 Read the tips. What is a minimalist?

Do you want to be a minimalist?

Can you live without a lot of possessions? Here's how to do it!

- Ask the questions: Is this **useful**?
- Do I really need it?
- Remember – you don't want a **messy** bedroom!
- Find **creative** ways to organize your things.
- Make it fun and **enjoyable** – have a 'throwing away' party.
- Be **realistic**! You can't keep everything!

2 Complete the table with the words in bold in exercise 1.

-able	*-ful*	*-ic*	*-ive*	*-y*
			creative	

3 Complete the words with suffixes. Add them to the table in exercise 2.

1 act-
2 help-
3 nois-
4 fashion-
5 artist-
6 stress-
7 luck-
8 athlet-
9 imaginat-
10 comfort-

4 35 Listen and check your answers to exercise 3.

5 Work in pairs. Complete the words with the correct suffix. Then ask and answer the questions.

1 Who is the most athlet _________ person you know? Who is the most artist _________ ?
2 What do you find stress _________ ? What do you find enjoy _________ ?
3 Is your bedroom mess _________ ? Is it nois _________?
4 Are you an imaginat _________ person or are you more realist _________ ?
5 Do you usually choose fashion _________ clothes or clothes that are comfort _________ ?

An interview

6 36 Listen to a radio interview with a teenage minimalist. Put the things in the order in which he talks about them.

a why he became a minimalist __
b how he feels now __
c how long he's been a minimalist __
d tips for becoming a minimalist __
e what he decided to keep __

Subskill: Justifying answers

Remember, when you answer true/false or yes/no questions, it's important to know why. Be prepared to explain your answers.

7 Listen again. Are the sentences true or false? Give reasons for your answers.

1 Ryan decided to become a minimalist three years ago.
2 He wanted to clean his room at the beginning of the school year.
3 He gave all the things that he didn't need to charity.
4 He kept some things from his childhood.
5 He has photos of some things he gave away.
6 He has more money now to buy new things.
7 He's never sorry after throwing away things.

8 Work in pairs. What could you live without? Follow the instructions below.

1 Individually, write a list of your possessions. You have three minutes.
2 Swap your list with your partner. Cross out all the things on your partner's list that you think aren't necessary.
3 Show the list to your partner again. Do you agree that the things aren't necessary? Give reasons for your answer.

Present perfect and simple past

1 **Read the examples. Which sentences are in the present perfect and which are in the simple past? How do you know?**

How long **have** you **been** a minimalist?
How **did** it **start**?
I'**ve been** a minimalist for about three years.
It was the end of the school year and I **wanted** to clean my room.
I'**ve done** that once or twice.

2 **Complete the rules with *present perfect* or *simple past*. Match the sentences in exercise 1 with the rules.**

1 We use the ________________ for unfinished actions in the past.
2 We use the ________________ for finished actions in the past.
3 We use the ________________ for actions that happened in the past without saying when.

3 **Circle the correct option.**

1 He **has sold/sold** a lot of his clothes three years ago.
2 I**'ve have/had** this watch since I was six.
3 We**'ve been/went** to California twice.
4 My parents **have taken/took** this photo last year.

4 **Complete the dialogues with the present perfect or simple past.**

A
How long **1** ________ **(you/ have)** those sneakers?
I **2** ________ **(have)** them for about a year. I **3** ________ **(buy)** them online.

B
When **4** ________ **(you / get)** that watch?
My parents **5** ________ **(give)** it to me for my birthday, but I **6** ________ **(not wear)** it before.

Time expressions

5 **Read the examples. Which time expressions do we often use with the present perfect? Which do we use with the simple past?**

A few years **ago**, Ryan decided to get rid of his things.
I've done this **for** three years.
I've had these comic books **since** 2017.
Last year, I threw away my skates.

6 **Copy and complete the table with the time expressions in the box.**

all my life for a month in 2020 in July
last summer last week since Monday
since I was six ~~three years ago~~ yesterday

Present perfect	Simple past
	three years ago

7 **Work in pairs. Ask how long your partner has had the things in the box.**

the clothes you're wearing your watch
your phone your backpack your sneakers

8 **Circle the correct option.**

GRAMMAR ROUND-UP
1 2 3 4 5 6 7 **8**

Celebrity shoes!

Most celebrities have a lot of clothes. In fact, they usually have **1** (...)! So they often give their old clothes and shoes to charities.

One of these charities is the Small Steps Project. Amy Hanson and her friends **2** (...) the idea for the project while they **3** (...) in Cambodia. They saw that people didn't have **4** (...) money to buy shoes, so they decided to help them.

Every year, the Small Steps Project **5** (...) a special event in London. They invite celebrities to come and sell their shoes. It's now the **6** (...) event of this type in the world, and the charity **7** (...) thousands of pounds since it started. One year, Emma Watson sold a pair of boots that she used **8** (...) for £6,000!

If you **9** (...) to their website, you'll see the shoes and how much people paid for them.

1	**a** too much	**b** too many	**c** enough
2	**a** have	**b** were having	**c** had
3	**a** work	**b** were working	**c** worked
4	**a** some	**b** a lot	**c** enough
5	**a** has	**b** is having	**c** was having
6	**a** large	**b** more important	**c** biggest
7	**a** is making	**b** made	**c** has made
8	**a** wear	**b** to wear	**c** to wearing
9	**a** will go	**b** go	**c** went

Reinforcement and Challenge Grammar bootcamp p126

Asking about lost and found objects

1 Work in pairs. Describe the objects in the photos. Use the words in the box.

hard heavy huge light medium-sized patterned plain round soft square tiny valuable

2 Watch the video. What did Louis leave in the café? Does he find it?

3 Watch again. Which Key phrases do you hear?

4 Complete the dialogue with the Key phrases. Watch again and check.

Louis Excuse me. I think I **1** ________ here. Have you seen it?

Waitress I don't think so. Where **2** ________ it?

Louis Over there, on the table in the corner. I was here just a few minutes ago.

Waitress What **3** ________ like?

Louis It's got a cover. It **4** ________ plastic.

Waitress What colour is it?

Louis It's **5** ________ , and it's got a pattern on it.

Waitress Right. What **6** ________ ?

Louis It's an iPhone. It's really important to me. I've had it for ages, and it's got all my stuff on it. Could you **7** ________ for it?

Waitress Just a moment. Is this it?

Louis Yes, it is. Phew! Thanks!

5 Create your own dialogue. Follow the steps in the Skills boost.

SKILLS BOOST

THINK

1 Choose an object in exercise 1, or your own.
2 Make notes to describe your object. Think about the material, color, make/brand and size.
3 Decide where you left the object (in a café, in the classroom, on the bus, etc.)

PREPARE

Prepare a dialogue.

PRACTICE

Practice your dialogue. Take turns asking about the lost object.

PERFORM

Act out your dialogue for the class.

6 **Peer review** Listen to your classmates. Answer the questions.

1 What did your classmates lose? Did they find it?
2 Which Key phrases did they use?

Key phrases

Asking about a lost object: What does it look like?
What's it made of?
What make/brand is it?
What color is it?
When did you lose it?
Where did you leave it?

Describing a lost object:
I think I left my ... here/on the bus/in classroom 7B.
Could you have a look for it?
It's quite big/small/medium-sized.
It's made of (plastic/wool/glass ...).

UK → US

Could you **have a look** for it? (UK) → Could you **take a look** for it? (US)
It's got a cover. (UK) → **It has** a cover. (US)

Jack To: Ollie Friday

Hi Ollie,

Thanks for a really great time last weekend. (Please say thank you to your parents again too.) The laser tag on Saturday afternoon was awesome and I really enjoyed the meal at your uncle's pizzeria in the evening. That was definitely the best I've ever had!

By the way, have you seen my watch anywhere? I think I left it in the bedroom. Could you take a look for it? If it isn't there, maybe I lost it playing laser tag. 😥 It's blue, it has a round face with white numbers on it and a plastic strap. I've had it since I was a kid, so I don't want to lose it – it's really special to me. Fingers crossed!

If you find it, don't worry about sending it to me. You could bring it when you come here next month.

Anyway, let me know.

See you soon!

Jack

A

B

C

A personal email

1 Read the email. Answer the questions.

1 What is Jack saying 'thank you' for?

2 What else does he write about?

2 Read the email again. Complete the sentences.

1 On Saturday afternoon, Jack and Ollie ______________________.

2 On Saturday evening, they ______________________.

3 Jack thinks that he left his watch ______________________.

4 Another possibility is that ______________________.

5 The watch is important to him because ______________________.

6 Ollie can bring the watch when he visits Jack ______________________.

3 Look at the photos. Which is Jack's watch?

4 Complete the table with adjectives to describe Jack's watch.

Opinion	Size	Shape	Age	Color	Material
special					

▶ Subskill: Adjective order

There is a special order for adjectives when we describe things: opinion, size, shape, age, color and material. We usually only use two or three adjectives to describe something.

5 Add the adjectives in the box to the table in exercise 4.

ancient cotton expensive fantastic
huge long new pink plastic
square tiny yellow

6 Write the adjectives in the correct order.

1 Last week, I bought a (...) dress. **(cotton, pink, cheap)** ______________

2 I left my (...) scarf at the swimming pool. **(wool, long, gray)** ______________

3 My friend has a (...) coin. **(silver, ancient, beautiful)** ______________

4 Have you seen my (...) sweater? **(blue, old, big)** ______________

5 My grandparents gave me a (...) watch for my last birthday. **(new, gold, fantastic)** ______________

6 I have a (...) alarm clock. **(green, small, square)** ______________

7 **Write an email to a friend or family member telling them about an object that you lost while you were with them. Follow the steps in the Skills boost.**

SKILLS BOOST

THINK

1 Choose a person to write to (a friend, aunt or uncle, cousin, grandparent, etc.).

______

2 What did you do when you visited them?

______

3 Choose an object that you lost.
- How did you lose it?

______

- Why is it important to you?

______

- How can you describe it?

______

PREPARE

Organize your notes into paragraphs.
- thank you
- the object
- how the person can return the object to you

______

WRITE

Write your email.

CHECK

Read your email and answer the questions.

1 Do you say thank you and write about a lost object? ☐

2 Do you use the present perfect and simple past correctly? ☐

3 Do you use adjectives to describe the object? Are they in the correct order? ☐

8 **Peer review** **Exchange your email with another student. What does the writer say 'thank you' for?**

Quick review

Grammar

Present perfect with *for* and *since*

We use the present perfect with *for* and *since* to talk about how long we have had something or have done something. The action is unfinished.

*I've **had** my watch **for** three years.*

*I've **been** a Liverpool fan **since** I was a kid.*

We use *since* when we say the beginning of the time period.

We use *for* when we say the duration of the time period.

*I've known Jack **for** six years.*

*I've known Jack **since** 2019.*

Time expressions

For: half an hour, two weeks, three years, a long time ...

Since: 2019, 2 o'clock, July, Friday, I was eight, breakfast ...

Present perfect and simple past

We use the present perfect to talk about unfinished actions in the past, or actions that happened in the past, but we don't say when.

We often use the present perfect with: *for* and *since*, *all my life*, etc.

*I've **lived** in this apartment **for** six years/**since** 2020/ **all my life**.*

We use the simple past to talk about finished actions in the past.

We often use the simple past with: *ago*, *last*, *in*, *yesterday*.

*We **moved** to this apartment six years **ago**/**last** September/**in** 2020.*

*I **did** my homework **yesterday**.*

Vocabulary

37 Describing things: materials

cotton, glass, gold, metal, paper, plastic, silver, wood, wool

38 Describing things: adjectives

hard, heavy, huge, light, medium-sized, patterned, plain, round, soft, square, tiny, valuable

39 Adjective suffixes

-able: comfortable, enjoyable, fashionable
-ful: helpful, stressful, useful
-ic: artistic, athletic, realistic
-ive: active, creative, imaginative
-y: lucky, messy, noisy

7 Project

WDYT?
(What do you think?)

How important are personal possessions?

TASK: Prepare a 'Me Box' and make a video of yourself talking about the items in it.

Learning outcomes

1 I can make a video about my important personal possessions.
2 I can work independently.
3 I can use appropriate language from the unit.

Graphic organizer → Project planner p133

1 Watch a video of a student presenting their box. What different objects does James have in his 'Me Box'?

STEP 1: THINK

2 Work in pairs. Look at James' notes in the Model project. What things does he include in his box?

1 things from different periods of his life (when?)
2 things that show what he loves and hates
3 handwritten letters, notes, poems, cards
4 things that help him remember a special event
5 clothes, toys, books
6 official documents: certificates, school grades, membership cards
7 things which are expensive or valuable
8 things related to his hobbies or interests

3 Look again at the Model project and answer the questions.

1 What information does James write about each item?
2 Does he write complete sentences or notes?

STEP 2: PLAN

4 Work individually. Think of items to include in your Me Box. Use the list in exercise 2 to help you.

5 Make a table with notes and information about each item.

STEP 3: CREATE

6 Work in pairs. Read the tips in the Super skills box and practice saying the Key phrases with your partner.

CREATIVITY — **SUPER SKILLS**

Taking the initiative

Tips

Organize your time – do your best work and don't leave things until the last minute.

Divide the task into steps (first: choose the objects, second: describe the objects, third: make the video, etc.).

Offer each other help to complete your individual projects.

Key phrases

What are the different steps?
We need to do this by next Friday.
First of all, we need to …
Why don't you send me your video when you've done it?
Then we need to …
I'll send you my video.
Should I text you tonight?

7 Work in pairs. Talk about how to organize your projects. Use the tips and Key phrases in the Super skills box.

Grammar and Vocabulary Quick review p93

Model project

Me Box

What?	How long?	Why?
sock	since I was a baby	so tiny! Was I really that small??
book	since my fourth birthday	favorite book when I was little
photo / Disneyland® Paris	for seven years	an amazing vacation with my family
a kiwi	for two days	I hate kiwis!!!
swimming goggles	for about a year	I ♥ swimming; train three times a week; compete with club
Harry Styles concert photo	since January	Jan 17th – amazing concert
my phone	for two years	the most expensive thing I have and the most important thing (friends, music, videos, games ...)

8 **Read the *How to ...* tips on p133. Then make a video of yourself talking about your Me Box.**

STEP 4: PRESENT

9 **Peer review** **Watch another student's video. As you watch, answer the questions.**

1. Does the speaker include a variety of possessions?
2. Do they say how long they've had the possession?
3. Do they explain the reason for including each item?
4. Do you learn anything new about the speaker?

7 FINAL REFLECTION

1 The task

Did you include a variety of possessions?

Did you explain clearly why each possession is important to you?

2 Super skill

Did you take initiative for your work?

Did you organize the work and complete it independently? Give examples.

3 Language

In your notes and video, did you use the language from the unit? Give examples.

8 Responsibility

WDYT?
(What do you think?)

What responsibilities do teenagers have?

Vocabulary: household chores; *-ed* and *-ing* adjectives

Grammar: *have to*; *will* and *going to*

Reading: an online news story about household chores

Listening: a presentation given by a teacher at an Open Day

Speaking: making offers and requests

Writing: a for-and-against essay

Project: plan a class for the end of the school year

Video skills p97

Real-world speaking p103

Project pp106–107

THIS WEEK'S CHORES

	Monday	Thursday	Saturday
Ali	load the dishwasher 	set the table 	do the laundry 
Samira	empty the dishwasher 	clear the table 	hang out the laundry 
Moeen	take out the trash 		iron the clothes 

Household chores

1 Who does each of these chores in your home?

1 make my bed ________
2 clean my room ________
3 make dinner ________
4 do the shopping ________
5 clean the bathroom ________
6 take care of my brother/sister ________

Verb forms

Remember that you sometimes need to change the form of verbs when you use them in a sentence.

2 Complete the sentences with the correct form of the verbs in exercise 1.

1 I always ________ my bed in the morning.
2 I usually ________ my room, but sometimes my mom ________ it.
3 My sister ________ dinner last night.
4 My dad ________ the shopping right now.
5 I ________ the bathroom last Saturday (but I hate doing it!).
6 My mom and dad ________ my brother and sister together.

George's chores

	Mon	Tues	Fri	Sat
take the dog for a walk		✓	✓	
sweep the floor	✓			
cut the grass				✓

3 Look at the chores charts. Who ... ?

1 sweeps the floor
2 sets the table
3 does the dishes
4 dries the dishes
5 does the laundry
6 hangs out the laundry
7 takes out the trash

4 Complete the sentences with the chores.

1 On Thursdays, Samira ________________ .
2 Valeria ________________ on Tuesdays and ________________ on Saturdays.
3 George ________________ twice a week.
4 Moeen ________________ on Saturdays.
5 On Mondays, Ali ________________ and Samira ________________ it.
6 José ________________ on Tuesdays and ________________ on Saturdays.
7 George ________________ on Saturdays.

5 Work in pairs. Look at categories 1–7 and write household chores for each one.

1 clothes
2 in the yard
3 before a meal
4 after a meal
5 cleaning
6 trash
7 with pets

clothes: do the laundry, ...

6 Work in groups of four. Ask each other about how often you do the household chores. Find out who does the most.

How often do you do the dishes?

I sometimes do it – maybe once or twice a week. I don't like doing it. What about you?

I never do it because we have a dishwasher.

VIDEO SKILLS

7 Watch the video. What different activities do you see?

8 Work in pairs. Discuss the questions.

1 Is this video ... ?
   a informative
   b entertaining
   c trying to sell something
2 Who do you think would like this video?
3 How does the vlogger make the video interesting? Think about:
   - humor
   - his voice
   - images
   - his facial expressions

An online news story

1 **Work in pairs. Write as many phrases describing household chores as you can using the words in the box. You have one minute!**

dishes dishwasher dusting floor iron laundry plants table trash

2 **Look at the photos in the news story and answer the questions.**

1 What chores can you see?
2 Are they the same or different in your country?

3 **Read the title of the news story. What do you think the answer is?**

4 **Read the news story quickly and answer the questions.**

1 Check your answer in exercise 3.
2 What household chores do the girls do?

5 40 **Read and listen to the news story. Are the sentences true or false? Why?**

1 Girls around the world spend 160 million hours a day helping at home.
2 Between the ages of ten and 14, they help for four hours a week.
3 Some girls help for more than 20 hours a week.
4 The girls spend most time taking care of their brothers and sisters.
5 Girls often have less time for homework than boys.
6 In the USA, boys and girls spend the same number of hours helping at home.

6 **Read the news story again. Find the phrases or sentences that mean the same.**

1 Sahra and Najma are similar to other girls in other countries.
2 Some girls help at home for more than nine hours.
3 They do chores that are hard work.
4 It's often easier for boys to get a good job and experience more things than girls.
5 The information in the report isn't necessarily true for girls in all countries.
6 There are advantages to doing household chores.

Subskill: Identifying text type

When you read a text, think about why the writer wrote it. Is the text for entertainment or to give facts? Is it fun or serious?

7 **Work in pairs. Discuss the questions.**

1 What is the purpose of the article? How do you know?
2 Where does the information come from?
3 Does the writer give an opinion in the text?

8 **Word work** **Match the definitions to the words in bold in the text.**

1 making better ________
2 things that everyone should have (legally or morally) ________
3 household chores, e.g. cleaning ________
4 the possibility that something will happen in the same way ________
5 an official document produced after studying a problem or situation ________
6 the possibilities or chances to do something ________

9 **Complete the sentences with words from exercise 8.**

1 My parents both do ________ . My dad cleans, and my mom does the laundry.
2 Good exam results give you better ________ .
3 Many organizations are ________ the lives of children around the world.
4 They did a lot of research before they wrote the ________ .
5 There is a ________ for parents to ask girls to help cook.
6 Most people agree that girls and boys have the same ________ .

CRITICAL THINKING — **SUPER SKILLS**

1 **Understand** What reasons are there for boys and girls to share household chores?
2 **Apply** Do you think that boys and girls do the same amount of housework in your country? What reasons are there for this?
3 **Create** What could you do to make sure that girls and boys spend the same amount of time helping at home?

CELEBRITY CORNER

Selena Gómez became a UNICEF ambassador in 2009. How old was she?

Do girls have to do more household chores?

Sahra is ten years old. Every morning, she wakes up early and bakes bread for her family's breakfast before she goes to school. Her 14-year-old sister Najma spends five hours a week washing the family's clothes.

Sahra and Najma live in Somalia, but they're typical of many girls around the world. According to a **report** by UNICEF*, girls around the world between the ages of five and 14 spend 40% more time helping at home than their brothers. In total, they do 550 million hours of housework a day – that's 160 million more hours than boys!

'Girls spend 160 million more hours doing housework every day than boys.'

Girls aged between five and nine spend an average of four hours a week on **housework**, while older girls spend about nine hours. In some countries, these numbers are even higher. In Somalia, for example, a girl between the ages of ten and 14 sometimes has to spend 26 hours a week helping at home.

The girls mainly help with cooking and cleaning. They also go shopping and take care of their younger brothers and sisters. In some countries, they also do heavy and dangerous chores such as collecting water and wood for making fires.

As a result, the report says, girls often don't have the same **opportunities** in life as boys. While their brothers are playing soccer outside, they have to sweep the floors. They don't have time to play, spend time with friends, or to study.

The report focuses on developing countries, but there is a similar **tendency** in other parts of the world. A study by the University of Maryland in the USA found that boys don't have to do as much housework as their sisters. On average, they spend about half an hour each day helping at home, compared to 45 minutes for girls.

The situation is **improving**: boys do more household chores now than they did in the past. But parents should make sure that children share housework equally. After all, doing housework can teach both boys and girls about responsibility, and this can help them at school and later at work.

Fact box

64% of girls help with the cooking and cleaning

50% go shopping

46% collect water or wood for fires

43% take care of other children

*UNICEF is an organization that protects children's **rights**.

have to

1 Read the examples. Circle the correct option to complete the rules.

They **have to** sweep the floors.
I **don't have to** collect water or firewood.
A girl **has to** spend 26 hours a week helping at home.

1 We use *have to* when something is **necessary/possible**.
2 We use *don't have to* when something is **prohibited/isn't necessary**.

2 Complete the table with the correct form of *have to*.

Affirmative		
I/you/we/they	1	sweep the floors.
he/she/it	2	help at home.
Negative		
I/you/we/they	3	collect water.
he/she/it	4	do much housework.

3 Complete the sentences with the affirmative or negative form of *have to*, and a verb in the box.

carry do get up set work

1 She ________ the table before dinner. **(+)**
2 I ________ early on the weekend. **(–)**
3 We ________ an English test every week. **(+)**
4 My dad ________ on the weekend. **(–)**
5 People in the UK ________ an identity card. **(–)**

must* and *have to

In the affirmative, *must* and *have to* are similar. In the negative, the meaning is different.
I **must / have to** do the dishes. = It's necessary.
I **don't have to** water the plants because it's raining. = It isn't necessary.
We **mustn't** talk during a test. = It's prohibited.

have to: questions

4 Look at the examples. Order the words in the box to make two correct question forms.

have to subject question word *do/does* base form

Do you **have to** help at home? No, I **don't**.
Does he **have to** clean? Yes he **does**.
What **do** you **have to** do?

5 Order the words to make questions.

1 you / do / help / at home / have to / when ?
2 your teacher / does / work / after school / have to ?
3 do / what time / have to / you / on Fridays / get up ?
4 you / have to / go to bed / do / at a particular time ?
5 your parents / have to / on Saturdays / work / do ?

6 Work in pairs. Ask and answer the questions in exercise 5.

7 Read the chat between a student in the USA and a student in Japan. Circle the correct option.

Zayn: Hey Kaito, is it true that students in Japan **1 have to/has to** clean their school?

Kaito: Yes, it is. We **2 not have to/don't have to** clean the restrooms, but we have **3 sweep/to sweep** the classroom floor every day. **4 Have you/Do you have** to clean your school too?

Zayn: No, we **5 haven't to/don't**!

Kaito: Here, it's normal. We have lunch in the classroom, and each student **6 has to/have to** take a cloth to school so that they can clean after they finish eating. The teacher **7 doesn't have to/don't have to** tell us to do it. It's part of our daily routine!

Zayn: Does your teacher **8 have to/has to** clean too?

Kaito: No, he **9 hasn't/doesn't**. Only the students do it. In Japan, it's part of our education to learn to keep places clean.

8 Answer the question to solve the Brain teaser.

BRAIN TEASER

Six students each do one chore at school. The boys' names are Dang, Andy, Justin and Luke. The girls' names are Daniela and Olivia. Read the clues. Make a list of the chores.

1 One of the girls has to clean the whiteboard. The other has to water the plants.
2 Dang, Andy and Justin don't have to close the windows.
3 Daniela and Andy and the girl who waters the plants are friends.
4 Justin, Olivia and Andy often walk home with the boy who has to take out the trash.
5 Andy doesn't have to sweep the floor.
6 Someone has to do the dusting.

What does each student do?

-ed and *-ing* adjectives

1 **Look at the information sheet. Who is it for?**

a students at Camworth High School now

b possible future students at Camworth High School

• CAMWORTH HIGH SCHOOL •

OPEN DAY – April 30th 6:00 pm

Starting at a new school isn't easy. It's normal to feel a little worried and nervous, but we are here to help you.

Changing school also gives you lots of exciting opportunities to do new things.

If you're interested in computers, you can join our Tech Club. If you like sports, Camworth High is the place to be: we have a fantastic gym and indoor swimming pool. If all those sports makes you feel exhausted, try something more relaxing like our yoga classes or the Photography Club.

You also have the chance to help in a local old people's home or be part of an environmental work group in Camworth Forest Park.

And don't forget our great team of teachers! Our students get excellent results on official exams.

2 **Complete the table with adjectives from the text. Then circle the correct option.**

-ed adjectives	*-ing* adjectives
worried	

1 Use adjectives ending in *-ed* to describe **things/how people feel**.

2 Use adjectives ending in *-ing* to describe **things/how people feel**.

3 **Match the adjectives in the box with definitions 1–7.**

annoyed challenging embarrassing exhausted satisfied tiring worried

1 happy that something you wanted happened or you did something well ________

2 unhappy because you are thinking about bad things that might happen ________

3 makes you feel shy or ashamed ________

4 very tired ________

5 a little angry ________

6 difficult, but makes you feel good ________

7 makes you want to rest or sleep ________

4 **Complete the sentences with the correct form of the adjectives in exercise 3.**

1 Keir is very good at ping-pong, so it was very ________ to win the game!

2 You always arrive late. It's so ________ !

3 I'm ________ about the exams. I don't think I'm ready!

4 Yesterday's training was completely ________ : it was three hours long and we didn't stop running.

5 I had to read aloud in French today in front of the class. It was horrible – I felt so ________ .

A presentation

Subskill: Recognizing feelings

You can understand how someone feels by listening to how they speak as well as what they say.

5 41 **Listen to the presentation Mrs. Reed gives at the Open Day.**

1 Is it about school subjects, sports or community action at the school?

2 How does Mrs. Reed feel about it?

FUN FACTS

In the UK many schools have prefects. These are older students who help to organize school events and set a good example for other students.

6 **Listen again and identify the incorrect information in each sentence.**

1 Mrs. Lopez is going to talk about the subjects you can study.

2 Students say this is one of the most boring things.

3 The teachers organized a quiz night.

4 Older students are running a clothes bank.

5 Year 8 students spend three Sundays working in the forest.

6 Maidment Court is a children's home.

7 **Listen again and correct the sentences in exercise 6.**

8 **Work in pairs. Discuss the questions.**

1 What type of extra activities can you take part in at your school?

2 Have you ever done any volunteer work? If so, what did you do and what did you learn from it? If not, what type of project would you like to work on?

will and *going to*

1 **Read the examples and circle the correct option to complete the rules.**

Mrs. Lopez is **going to** tell you about sports.
Are you **going to** tell us about working in the Forest Park?
I'll tell you about that in just a minute.

1 We use auxiliary ***be/do*** + *going to* + base form.
2 After *will* we use the **infinitive/base form.**
3 The difference between *will* and *going to* is **when the future action happens/when we decide to do the future action**.
4 We use ***will/going to*** for things we have planned or know about before we say them.
5 We use ***will/going to*** for spontaneous decisions, made at the time of speaking.

Present progressive for plans

We also use the present progressive to talk about more definite plans or arrangements (e.g. when you have bought a ticket).
My mom's flying back from Copenhagen tonight.

2 **Complete the sentences with the correct form of *going to* and a verb in the box.**

buy do eat study visit

1 My brother ________________ engineering in college next year. He loves robots.
2 I've decided I ________________ those shoes. They're too expensive.
3 We ________________ my grandparents this weekend.
4 ________________ that cake or can I have it?
5 What ________________ on the weekend?

3 **Ask your partner questions. Use *What are you going to do ... ?* and a time expression in the box.**

after class after school today
next weekend on the next break
this evening when you leave school

What are you going to do after school today?

I'm going to do my homework.

4 **Match the sentences to make short dialogues.**

1 I can't carry all these books.
2 Look outside, it's raining.
3 We don't have any eggs.
4 I'm really worried about tomorrow's exam.

a I'll help you study.
b I'll take an umbrella.
c I'll go and buy some.
d I'll help you with them.

5 **Complete the dialogue using *will* or *going to* and the verbs in parentheses.**

I **1** ________________ **(watch)** a movie at home tonight. Do you want to come?

What **2** ________________ **(you/watch)** ?

Ragnarok. I love the Thor movies!

OK, I **3** ________________ **(come)** over at 8 then.

My mom **4** ________________ **(order)** a pizza. I **5** ________________ **(ask)** her to get a family-sized one.

Great! I **6** ________________ **(bring)** some orange juice.

6 **Circle the correct option.**

GRAMMAR ROUND-UP

1 2 3 4 5 6 7 8

Sixteen-year-old Brandon Donnelly **1 has won/won** Sport Scotland's Young Volunteer of the Year award in 2017. Brandon **2 spends/is spending** several hours a week working for the PEEK charity with children in Calton, Glasgow, organizing play sessions and soccer in streets and local parks. Brandon thinks that if children **3 plays/play** sports, they will become **4 healthier/the healthier** adults and live longer.

Brandon has been part of PEEK **5 for/since** he was five years old, when he **6 used to/use to** take part in play sessions himself.

Brandon **7 mustn't/doesn't** have to volunteer, but he enjoys it and he also says he is now more confident and organized. He says he **8 will/is going to** work with children when he is older.

Making offers and requests

1 Watch the video. Jen has been off school sick for a week. What does she ask Rob to do?

2 Watch again. Which Key phrases do you hear?

3 Complete the dialogue with the correct base form or infinitive verb. Watch again and check.

Rob Hi Jen. Are you feeling better?

Jen Yes, a little. Listen, I have to catch up on the math lessons you did in class last week. Could you **1** ________ me a hand?

Rob Yeah, no problem.

Jen Can you **2** ________ me what pages you did?

Rob Let's see ... we started Unit 5 – algebra. Would you like me **3** ________ you my notes?

Jen That would be great, thanks.

Rob And we did a new type of equation. Shall I **4** ________ you later?

Jen No, don't worry. I can **5** ________ by myself first.

Rob OK, well if you have any questions, I'm happy **6** ________ . Just ask.

Jen Sounds good. I'll do that.

Rob Well, take care of yourself.

Jen OK, thanks.

4 Create your own dialogue. Follow the steps in the Skills boost.

SKILLS BOOST

THINK
Think of a situation when you might offer to help a classmate or friend.

PREPARE
Prepare a dialogue. Remember to include Key phrases to make offers and requests.

PRACTICE
Practice your dialogue.

PERFORM
Act out your dialogue for the class.

5 **Peer review** Listen to your classmates and answer the questions.

1 What characteristics of a good classmate did they show?
2 Which Key phrases did they use?

Key phrases

Offering: Why don't I ... ?
Would you like me to ... ?
Shall I ... ?
What can I do now?
I'm happy to help.

Accepting/refusing an offer: Yes, great.
Sounds good.
That would be great, thanks.
It's alright, I'll do that.
No, don't worry, I can (do that).

Making a request: Could you ... ?
Can you ... ?

Agreeing to/refusing a request: Sure.
Yeah, no problem.
I'd rather not.
Could I do (...) instead?

US → UK

Yes, a little. (US) → Yes, a bit. (UK)
I have to catch up on the math. (US) → I have to catch up on the maths. (UK)

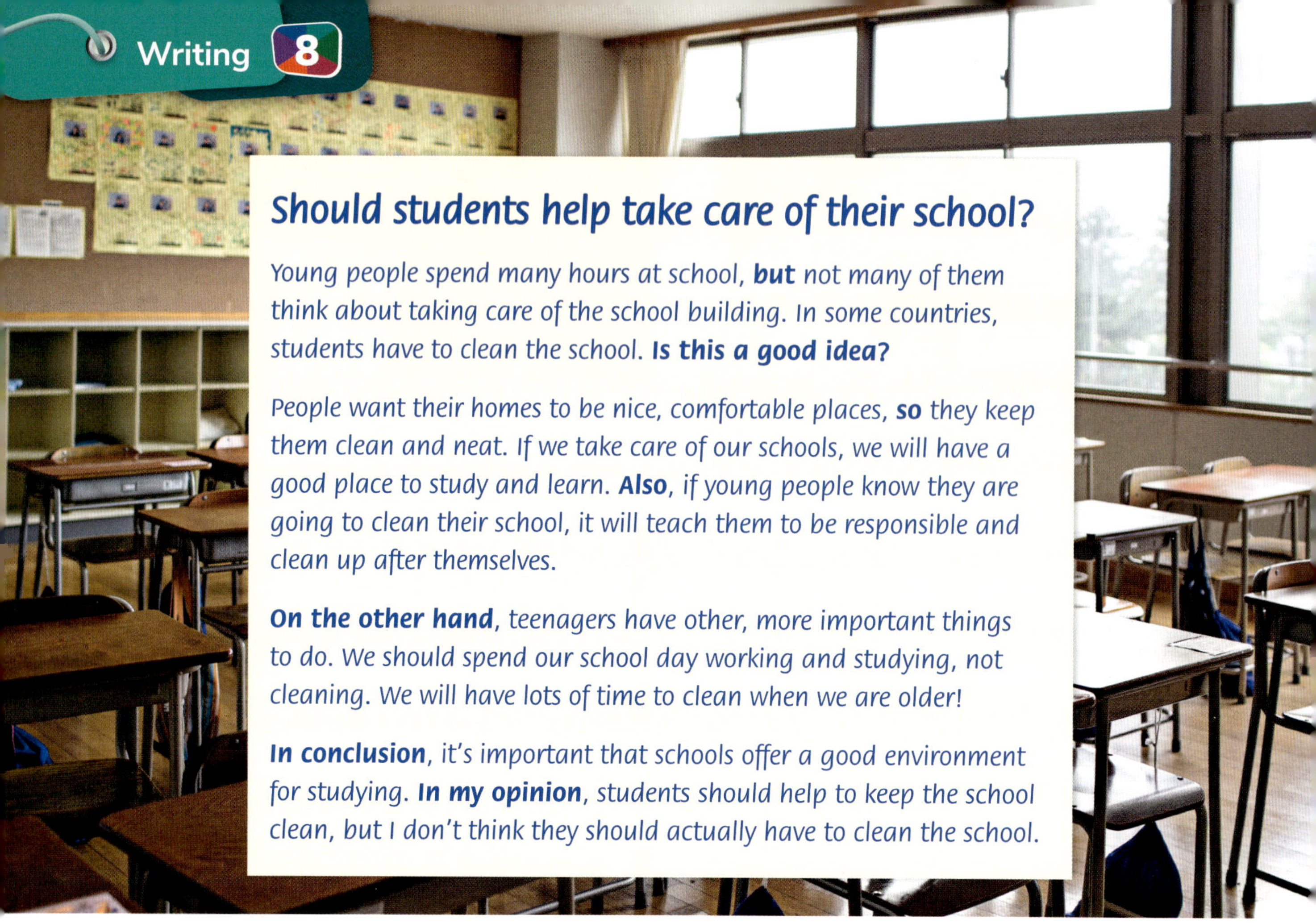

Should students help take care of their school?

Young people spend many hours at school, ***but*** *not many of them think about taking care of the school building. In some countries, students have to clean the school.* ***Is this a good idea?***

People want their homes to be nice, comfortable places, ***so*** *they keep them clean and neat. If we take care of our schools, we will have a good place to study and learn.* ***Also****, if young people know they are going to clean their school, it will teach them to be responsible and clean up after themselves.*

On the other hand*, teenagers have other, more important things to do. We should spend our school day working and studying, not cleaning. We will have lots of time to clean when we are older!*

In conclusion*, it's important that schools offer a good environment for studying.* ***In my opinion****, students should help to keep the school clean, but I don't think they should actually have to clean the school.*

A for-and-against essay

1 **Read the title and the essay. What is the writer's opinion on the title question?**

2 **Look at the essay and number the features in the correct order.**

- a Arguments against students helping to clean their school ___
- b Conclusion and personal opinion ___
- c Introduction ___
- d Title ___
- e Arguments for students helping to clean their school ___

3 **Find two arguments for helping to clean the school and two arguments against.**

4 **Match the expressions in bold in the essay to reasons why we use them 1–7.**

1. to ask a question to introduce the subject
2. to give a personal opinion
3. to introduce a contrast in a new paragraph
4. to introduce the final paragraph
5. to introduce a contrast in the same sentence
6. to introduce a result after giving reasons
7. to add an additional argument

▶ Subskill: Balancing arguments

When you write an essay, remember to include phrases to contrast ideas, to connect similar ideas or to add information.

5 **Complete the text using the expressions in bold in the essay.**

Should every family have a pet?

Some parents think pets are a lot of work. Other people say every family should have a pet;
1 ________________ ?
It's fun to take care of pets, but they can 2 ________________ teach you things. If you have a fish for example, you have to feed it and clean the tank. 3 ________________ this is a great way for children to learn to be responsible.
4 ________________ , pets take up a lot of time and they can be expensive. And what do you do with them when you go on vacation?
5 ________________ , animals can bring you lots of happiness 6 ________________ , they are also a big responsibility. 7 ________________ , you should think very carefully before you decide to get a pet.

6 Write a for-and-against essay on the subject 'Should teenagers have to help at home?' Follow the steps in the Skills boost.

SKILLS BOOST

THINK

With a partner, think of as many arguments as possible for and against teenagers helping at home.

for	against

PREPARE

1 Select two arguments for and two against to include in your essay.

2 Complete the sentence with your own opinion on the subject.

In my opinion ...

WRITE

Individually, write your essay. Use the models in exercises 1 and 5 to help you.

Many teenagers today ...

CHECK

Read your essay and answer the questions.

1 Do you organize your essay into four paragraphs? ☐

2 Do you include two arguments for and two arguments against? ☐

3 Do you give your own opinion in the final paragraph? ☐

4 Do you use expressions to connect your writing? ☐

5 Do you use *have to*? ☐

7 **Peer review** **Exchange your essay with other students. Do you agree with the writer's personal opinion?**

Quick review

Grammar

Obligation

must and *mustn't*

We use *must* + base form to express obligation, often from the speaker.

*You **must** work harder.*

We use *mustn't* + base form to express prohibition.

*You **mustn't run** beside the swimming pool.*

have to and *don't have to*

We use *have* + *to* + base form to express obligation which comes from rules or is passed on by the speaker.

*You **have to wear** a helmet when you bike.*

We use *don't have* + *to* + base form when something is optional and there is no obligation.

*You **don't have to come** if you don't want to.*

will and *going to*

Use *will* + base form to talk about a future action you decide when you are speaking.

***I'll come** with you.*

Use *going to* + base form to talk about a planned future, which you decide before speaking.

***I'm going to visit** Kelly in the hospital.*

Vocabulary

42 Household chores

clean the bathroom, clean your room, cut the grass, do the dishes, do the dusting, do the laundry, do the shopping, dry the dishes, feed the goldfish, hang out the laundry, iron the clothes, load/empty the dishwasher, make dinner, make your bed, set/clear the table, sweep the floor, take care of (your brother or sister), take out the trash/the recycling, take the dog for a walk, water the plants

43 *-ed* and *-ing* adjectives

annoyed / annoying
confused / confusing
embarrassed / embarrassing
excited / exciting
exhausted / exhausting
frightened / frightening
interested / interesting
relaxed / relaxing
satisfied / satisfying
tired / tiring
worried / worrying

8 Project

WDYT?
(What do you think?)

What responsibilities do teenagers have?

TASK: Make a proposal for the final class at the end of the school year.

Learning outcomes

1 I can take responsibility for planning a class.

2 I can think about the interests of other people.

3 I can use appropriate language from the unit.

Graphic organizer → Project planner p133

1 Watch a video of students presenting their proposal. What is their idea for the final class?

STEP 1: THINK

2 Look at the poster in the Model project. Which questions does it answer?

1 What is the idea?
2 When are you going to do it?
3 How are you going to organize it?
4 How will you practice English?
5 Who is going to be responsible for the preparation?
6 Will students need to bring things from home? What?
7 Where will you do it?

3 Make a list of ideas for the final class.

a treasure hunt *a quiz* *a video*

STEP 2: PLAN

4 Work in groups. Read the tips in the Super skills box and practice saying the Key phrases with your group.

CRITICAL THINKING — SUPER SKILLS

Thinking about other people's interests

Tips

Don't simply choose your personal preference, think about other options.

Think about advantages and disadvantages of different ideas.

Ask what most people will prefer.

Key phrases

I know you like ..., but ...

I think only a few people will want to do that.

We have to think about what other people want.

That's a nice idea, but it's difficult to organize.

Most people like ...

I think that's best for everyone.

5 In your group, choose one idea in exercise 3 to make a proposal for how to spend the final class at the end of the school year.

1 Include answers to the questions in exercise 2.
2 Think of reasons to explain your decisions. Make sure your proposal is fun, but easy to organize. Remember that you must use English in the class.
3 Use the tips and Key phrases in the Super skills box.

STEP 3: CREATE

6 Choose a format (poster, slideshow) and create the presentation for your proposal.

7 Practice giving your presentation.

Grammar and Vocabulary Quick review p105

Model project

STEP 4: PRESENT

8 Peer review **Read the How to ... tips on p133 and present your proposal to the class. As you listen to your classmates, answer the questions.**

1. Is their idea fun, easy to organize and useful?
2. How will students practice English in the class?
3. Do you think everyone would enjoy the activity? Give reasons for your answer.
4. Choose the best idea for the final class.

8 FINAL REFLECTION

1 **The task**
Does your plan include all the important points (how, why, etc.)?

2 **Super skill**
Do you think about the interests of other people? Give examples.

3 **Language**
In your presentation, do you use language from the unit? Give examples.

REVIEW Look what you know!

Vocabulary

1 **Name the things you can see in the photos.**

2 **For each word in exercise 1, write the letter indicated. Can you discover the missing word?**

1	2	3	4	5	6	7	8	9
5th	1st	4th	5th	2nd	1st	3rd	5th	2nd
o								

3 **Add three related words to each word in exercise 1. If you need help, look at topics 1–9.**

1 Unit 1: TV, movies, and games
2 Unit 5: your environment
3 Unit 4: money
4 Unit 5: rooms
5 Unit 2: everyday objects
6 Unit 5: furniture
7 Unit 7: describing things
8 Unit 6: music
9 Unit 2: life events

4 **Which verb can you use with all three of the expressions?**

1 the shopping, a bungee jump, the dusting
2 popular, famous, on TV
3 a job, good grades, fit
4 a race, a prize, a game

5 **Add a word from the box to each of the groups in exercise 4.**

born   a competition   married   the dishes

6 **Work in pairs. Complete the questions with the words in exercise 5. Then ask your partner.**

1 What do you think is the ideal age to get ________ ?
2 Have you ever won ________ ?
3 Which do you prefer: cleaning your room or doing ________ ?
4 Where were you ________ ?

7 **Complete the dialogue with the words in the correct form.**

A: I hear you did a bungee jump last weekend?

B: Yes, my dad saw some **1** ________ **(inform)** about this new place where you can jump off a bridge.

A: Was it an **2** ________ **(enjoy)** experience or was it too terrifying?

B: Well, I was really **3** ________ **(excite)** the day before, but when I was standing up on the bridge, I suddenly felt very **4** ________ **(frighten)**. But the guides were very **5** ________ **(help)** and explained everything very **6** ________ **(clear)**. And then I jumped and it was amazing!

A: How do you feel about it now?

B: I think it was a real **7** ________ **(achieve)**. I think it was one of the most **8** ________ **(satisfy)** things I've ever done.

Reading

1 **Match 1–3 with a–c to make sentences. They give advice from the Subskills in Units 1–8.**

1 When reading quickly, try to keep your eyes moving; ...

2 When you read for facts and numbers, look ...

3 The words in a question might be different from the text, ...

a so look for words with a similar meaning.

b don't stop when you see a word you don't know.

c quickly to find the information. Then check slowly.

2 **Look at the titles of the news stories. With a partner predict three items of vocabulary you think will be in each story.**

A Engineers today discover work from the past

B Swimming with dolphins or buying the latest phone?

C Plastic or prison?

D 3D printing saves lives

3 **Read the news stories quickly (Tip 1) and match them with titles A–D in exercise 2.**

4 **What does each number from the texts refer to? (Tip 2)**

1 3	**2** 30	**3** 32	**4** 22,000
5 10	**6** 57	**7** 4	

5 44 **Read and listen to the text. Are the sentences true or false? (Tip 3)**

1 All survey participants were the same nationality.

2 More than half of the people who answered the survey in Mexico said that experiences are more important.

3 3D printing has many different uses.

4 The doctors used bones from another part of the woman's body.

5 While engineers were making a new building, they discovered some historical objects.

6 They found some plates from five centuries ago.

7 Plastic bags are dangerous for ocean life.

8 If you use a plastic bag in Kenya, you might go to prison.

Exam tip

Don't panic if there's a word you don't know. Use the context (the situation and the words near it) to get an idea of the meaning.

6 **Word work** **The words in bold in the text all appeared in the Word work exercises in Units 1–8. Can you remember what they mean?**

1 ______

What's **worth** more to you: experiences or money? Some people say if you have money, you can buy the things you want. Others think experiences are better. Things break or get old, but memories of our experiences stay with us. In a recent survey, 22,000 participants in 5 **continents** were asked if they agreed or disagreed that: 'Experiences are more important than possessions.' And in Mexico, the highest proportion - 57% - agreed.

2 ______

We all know that the **research** into 3D printing is going to change things in the future. People are already using it to make houses, cars and shoes. But hospital teams are also using 3D printing. Doctors in Gurgaon, India, recently saved the life of a young teacher using 3D technology. They made three **artificial** bones for her back, and after just ten days the woman could walk again.

3 ______

Work on a new subway line in Rome has given engineers opportunities to find many interesting and **valuable** historical objects 30 meters down. Sixteenth-century plates, a 2nd-century building and even part of Rome's first university are a few of the things they have discovered.

4 ______

Plastic bags are not **environmentally friendly**. On average, we use them for only 12 minutes, but they kill about 100,000 marine animals every year. It's no surprise that 32 countries (a lot of them in the **developing world**) have decided to ban plastic bags completely. In Kenya people who make, sell or import plastic bags can go to prison for up to four years.

Grammar

The questions around the edge of the page will help you remember the grammar studied in the book. First answer the red questions from around the page. Next, do the exercises in the central red section. Then do the same with yellow, orange, green, blue and purple.

4 Circle the correct option.

*My friends and I decided yesterday that we'**ll/re** going to play football on Saturday.*

4 Circle the correct option.

***I've played/ played** tennis yesterday.*

4 Correct the sentence.

If it'll be sunny tomorrow, we'll go to the beach.

4 Is the meaning the same or different?

I'm older than my cousin. My cousin isn't as old as me.

4 Is the sentence correct or incorrect?

I was meeting an old friend while I was shopping yesterday.

4 Is the sentence correct or incorrect?

I read a good book right now.

1 Write the sentences in the simple present with the adverb of frequency or frequency expression.

1 He / do / karate **(twice a week)**
2 I / go / to the library **(hardly ever)**
3 Our teacher / not give / us homework **(every day)**
4 They / be / late for class **(always)**
5 We / not / have / an English test **(every week)**
6 My sister / clean / her room **(never)**

2 Complete the text with the simple present or present progressive.

Mason Coutinho is a teenage singer who **1** ______________ **(write)** his own songs. What **2** ______________ **(he/work)** on right now? Well, he **3** ______________ **(make)** an album. His brother **4** ______________ **(usually/not sing)** with him, but he **5** ______________ **(sing)** on this album.

What **6**______________ **(Mason/like)** doing when he **7**______________ **(not work)**? Well, apparently, he **8** ______________ **(not have)** a lot of free time, but he and his brother often **9** ______________ **(play)** basketball.

1 Circle the correct option.

1 My aunt **was/were** a journalist before she **become/became** a writer.
2 **You watched/Did you watch** TV last night?
3 I **can't/couldn't** swim until I was seven.
4 We used **walk/to walk** to elementary school every day.

2 Complete the sentences with the simple past or past progressive form of the verbs in the box.

arrive get on realize take off travel wait walk wear

Something unlucky happened while I **1** ________ to Bilbao last year. I **2** ________ the bus and I put my jacket on the seat. While we **3** ________ to leave, a boy sat down next to me. He also **4** ________ his jacket and put it on the seat. A few hours later, we **5** ________ in Bilbao. While I **6** ________ home, I **7** ________ that I **8** ________ the boy's jacket!

1 Are the sentences correct or incorrect? Correct the incorrect sentences.

1 I don't have many money with me.
2 There aren't some cafés near school.
3 Jenny buys a lot of new books.
4 How much people were there at the concert?
5 There aren't bike lanes enough in our town.

2 Complete the second sentence so that it means the same as the first. Use the word in parentheses.

1 Japanese is more difficult than English. **(easy)**
English ______________ Japanese.
2 London is more expensive than other cities in the UK. **(the)**
London is ______________ city in the UK.
3 The USA isn't as big as Canada. **(big)**
Canada ______________ the USA.
4 Trains are faster than buses. **(as)**
Buses aren't ______________ trains.

3 Order the words to make a sentence.

is / study / my / math / to / sister / at college / going

3 What's the question?

I've lived here for three years.

3 What type of conditional sentence is this?

If we heat ice, it changes to water.

3 Write the comparative and superlative of the adjectives.

old, funny, beautifu

What form of a verb do we use after *love/like/hate?* **1**

Write the sentence in the past.
There aren't any planes, so people can't fly. **1**

Which option is not correct? Why?
*I don't have **any/much/many** video games.* **1**

Write the negative of the sentence.
People will live on the Moon in 2030. **1**

1 Make predictions about the future with *will/won't* or *might*.

1 We / not be / in this class ten years from now (I'm sure)
2 Some of us / live / in another country (I'm sure)
3 I / go / to college (it's possible)
4 I / not work / in an office (I'm sure)
5 Some students / get married (I'm sure)
6 We / not have / houses on the Moon (I'm sure)
7 I / be rich and famous one day (it's possible)

2 Match 1–5 with a–e and write the verb in the correct form.

1 My grandmother is always happy
2 If it's sunny next weekend,
3 We won't be late
4 We'll be sad
5 If you aren't on time,
a if our team ________ **(not win)** the game.
b when she ________ **(see)** me.
c we ________ **(go)** to the park.
d if the bus ________ **(come)** soon.
e we ________ **(not wait)** for you.

Write a complete sentence in the present perfect. **1**
I / never / ride / a horse

They have to wear a school uniform. **1**
Can they wear jeans to school?

What is the negative of the sentence? **2**
He watches TV every day.

Write the simple past of these verbs. **2**
play, see, go, work, write

He doesn't have enough money to buy a laptop. **2**
Can he buy a laptop?

*It **will/might** rain tomorrow.* **2**
Which means it's a possibility?

1 Correct the sentences.

1 I've never eat Indian food.
2 You have ever stayed in a five-star hotel?
3 My dad has gone to Brazil many times.
4 How many time have you had those sneakers?
5 My mom's been a lawyer during 16 years.
6 My grandparents have ever traveled to another country.

2 Complete the dialogues with the present perfect or simple past.

1 ________ **(you / see)** the new Superman movie?
Yes, I ________ **(see)** it two weeks ago. I really ________ **(enjoy)** it!
2 What ________ **(you / do)** last weekend?
We ________ **(play)** laser tag. ________ **(you / try)** it?
3 ________ **(your brother / ever / go)** to London?
Yes, he ________ **(go)** there last year, but he ________ **(not like)** the cold weather.
4 How long ________ **(you / have)** that phone?
Since September. My parents ________ **(give)** it to me for my birthday.

1 Write sentences with *have to/has to* or *don't/doesn't have to* so that they are true for your school.

1 We / wear / a uniform
2 We / buy / our own textbooks
3 We / stand up / to answer a question
4 The cafeteria / serve / healthy food
5 Students / go outside / at break time
6 The teacher / clean / the classroom

2 Circle the correct option.

A: What **will you do/are you going to do** on Saturday?
B: I'm not sure. I**'ll probably/'m going to** study.
A: Paul and I **will/are going to** play football in the park.
B: In that case, I**'ll/'m going to** come with you. It**'ll be/'s going to be** more fun than studying!

Write the sentence in the negative. **3**
People used to have cell phones.

Order the words to make a sentence. **3**
I / to the movie theater / go / hardly ever

Write the sentence in the negative. **2**
My brother has to do homework.

Anke has been to Italy. **2**
Is Anke in Italy now?

Listening

1 **Work in pairs. Make a list of all the things that you listen to on a typical day.**

> **Remember!**
> You can understand better if you know what kind of thing you are listening to, e.g. a presentation, a conversation, a radio show, etc.

2 45 **Listen to five short extracts. What type of listening is each one?**

a conversation | a live report on TV | a podcast | a presentation | a recorded message | a teacher speaking to a class

3 46 **Listen to the complete extracts. Are the sentences true or false? Give reasons for your answers.**

1 The computer museum is open on Mondays.
2 Don Chang and Jin Sook Chang opened their first store in 1981.
3 The people are growing food in the city center.
4 Tushar Lakhanpal has 25,000 pencils in his collection.
5 The boy has to turn off his phone when he's having dinner.

4 **Work in pairs. Answer the questions.**

1 What do you expect to see at the computer museum?
2 Where in your city could you grow food?
3 What rules do you have about using a cell phone at home?

5 **You're going to listen to a podcast about music. Look at the photos and make a list of words that you expect to hear.**

> **Exam tip**
> Think about why sentences are incorrect. This will help you to choose the correct answer.

6 47 **Listen and circle the correct option.**

1 When the singers in the choir sing ...
  a they are all in different places.
  b they are online at the same time.
  c the composer uses technology to sing to them.
2 The choir started after ...
  a a girl wrote about the idea on her blog.
  b the composer posted a song online.
  c a fan sent a video to the composer.
3 The Virtual Youth Choir ...
  a sings in Scotland.
  b has more than 2,000 singers.
  c has singers from 100 countries.
4 Gómez decided to make a musical instrument ...
  a while he was looking in waste materials.
  b when he saw an old pizza pan.
  c because he didn't have enough money to buy a violin.
5 The 'trash' orchestra has ...
  a made more than 44 albums.
  b played in many different countries.
  c been on a tour in the USA with the band Metallica.
6 The 'trash' orchestra is important because ...
  a a lot of young people like traveling.
  b some musicians didn't play an instrument before.
  c now there are similar orchestras in other countries.

7 **Listen again and check your answers.**

8 **Work in pairs. Which story did you find most interesting? Why?**

Real-world speaking

1 **Work in pairs. In what situations do you ... ?**

1 describe an object
2 ask for and check information
3 talk about your experience and abilities

2 **Copy and complete the table with the Key phrases.**

Key phrases

Could you say that again?
How can I get there?
Do you know how to play any other instruments?
Do you have any experience playing in a band?
It's made of cotton. It's medium-sized.
Sorry, I didn't get that.
What does it look like?

Describing an object	Asking for clarification	Asking about experience

3 **Match A–E with the headings in the box.**

Making decisions Giving advice
Talking about preferences
Making offers and requests Telling a story

A
Would you rather watch a movie or play my new game?
I think **1** ________________ play your game. It sounds more fun.

B
Did I tell you about the time I lost my wallet?
No, I don't think so. **2** ________________ !

C
I want to buy a new phone, but I don't have any money.
3 ________________ do some extra household chores.

D
4 ________________ giving Mom a scarf for her birthday?
I'm not sure. She has a lot of scarves.

E
5 ________________ load the dishwasher?
No, don't worry, I can do that.

4 48 **Complete the dialogues in exercise 3 with the phrases in the box. Then listen and check.**

I'd prefer to ... What a nightmare!
What do you think about ...
Would you like me to ... You should ...

Exam tip
Learn complete phrases and try to use them in your speaking exams.

5 **Work in pairs. Prepare a dialogue for one of the situations. Follow the steps in the Skills boost.**

A **Organize an activity to celebrate the end of the year.**
B **Role-play an interview to work at a summer camp.**
C **Talk about ways to earn money during the summer break.**

SKILLS BOOST

THINK
Choose a situation.

PREPARE
Write your dialogue. Include six Key phrases.

PRACTICE
Practice your dialogue. Try to remember it.

PERFORM
Act out your dialogue for the class.

6 Peer review **Listen to your classmates and answer the questions.**

1 Which task did they choose?
2 Which Key phrases did they use?

Writing

1 Read texts A–D. What type of text are they?

A

Are summer breaks too long?

In some countries, schools close for two months in the summer. Most of us love having long vacations, but is this a good idea?

On the one hand, students work hard during the school year, and we need time to relax. The summer is a good time to do activities such as sports or volunteering. It's also difficult to study in August because of the weather.

B

Teen Titans Go! To the Movies, is one of my favorite movies. It tells the story of Robin, who wants to have his own superhero movie. The other superheroes say he isn't important enough.

I love this movie because it's really funny, and it teaches an important lesson about what it means to be a hero as well.

★★★★

C

Dear Jodi,

I'm having a great time here in Malibu. We're staying in a beautiful apartment near the beach. I'm spending most of my time sunbathing and swimming in the ocean, but I've tried surfing too (this is a great place for water sports like kitesurfing and sailing).

Jodi Larter
15 Main Street
Milwaukee, WI
53202

D

Deniz: Hey Tomas, could you take a look for my pencil case? I think I left it in the classroom. It's a square black case with a logo on the front. It's a little old, but it's my favorite. If you find it, can you send me a message?

2 Work in pairs. Take the quiz. Use the texts in exercise 1 to help you.

WHAT DO YOU REMEMBER?

1. We use *as well* when we add extra information. What two other words can we use? (2 POINTS)
2. Which two of the ways in 1 above comes at the end of a sentence? (1 POINT)
3. We use *because* and *because of* when we give a reason. Which do we use before a noun? (1 POINT)
4. We use *for example*, when we give examples. What are two other ways to give examples? (2 POINTS)
5. We use *who*, *which* and *where* to connect two sentences. Which do we use for places? (1 POINT)
6. We use *too* + *adjective* to say that something is more than we need. What is the opposite? (2 POINTS)
7. We use *Hi* and *Hey* to start a message or postcard. What other word can we use? (1 POINT)

TOTAL ... / 10 POINTS

How many of the words and phrases can you find in the texts in exercise 1?

3 Choose one task and write your answer in 140 words. Follow the steps in the Skills boost.

A **Write an email to a friend during the summer break.** Tell your friend about the things that you have done since the start of the vacation.

B **Write a for-and-against essay.** *Should students play sports in school? Discuss.*

C **Write a story for a writing competition.** Describe a time that you found an object. What was it? What did you do with it?

Exam tip

It's important to take time to plan ideas and language before you start writing.

SKILLS BOOST

THINK

1. Make notes about the information to include and think about the verb tenses.
2. Look again at the writing tasks in the book. Find words and phrases you can use.

PREPARE

Organize your writing into paragraphs.

WRITE

Write your email, essay or story.

CHECK

Read your writing. Answer the questions.

1. Do you use a variety of tenses and vocabulary?
2. Do you use words and phrases from the writing pages?
3. Can you find any mistakes?

4 Peer review **Work in groups. Read your classmates' writing and make a suggestion to make it better.**

REVIEW GAME

Key phrases:

You start.
Whose turn is it?
It's your/my turn.
Oh no, a snake! Bad luck!
A ladder! Lucky you!

How to play the SNAKES AND LADDERS game

1. Form groups of three to five students.
2. Each student needs a different coin or marker. Put these on START.
3. Take turns to roll a dice, move forward and follow the instructions on the square.
4. If you land on a ladder, you can climb up to the square at the top of it.
5. If you land on a snake, you have to follow the instructions on the square, then go down to the bottom of its tail.
6. The winner is the first to finish!

24 FINISH

23 Tell the group what you are going to do after class today.

22 Tell the group about an experience you have had.

21 Say three ways things were different in the past. Use *There was(n't) /were(n't)*.

17 Say something you're crazy about and explain why.

18 Tell the group about a brand you like and why.

19 Say four things you can find in a kitchen.

20 You have one minute. How many pieces of furniture can you name?

16 Say four adverbs.

15 Say something that you think will definitely happen next year and something that might happen.

14 What were you doing at 2 pm last Saturday?

13 You have one minute. How many materials can you name?

9 Say four words related to music.

10 Give someone in your group some advice about money.

11 Tell the group about something you aren't very interested in and explain why.

12 Tell the group about the last time you went to a party.

8 Ask each person in your group a different question.

7 Describe an object you can see in the classroom (material, size, shape ...).

6 What were you doing at 8:00 pm yesterday evening?

5 Say four adjectives.

1 START

2 Tell the group about your favorite TV series.

3 You have one minute. How many household chores can you name?

4 Tell the group about the last time you went to the movie theater.

Grammar bootcamp

Starter unit

Possessive adjectives

1 **Match 1–5 to a–e.**

1 Hi. I'm Milo! __
2 This is my sister. __
3 The tall one is my brother. __
4 These are my parents. __
5 This is Kieran's pet snake. __

a Their names are Pippa and Ben.
b Her name is Beth.
c Meet my family.
d Its name is Nagini.
e His name's Kieran.

have got

2 **Circle the correct option.**

1 My best friend **have/has** got two brothers: Dominic and Michael.
2 I love swimming, but we **haven't got/not have got** a pool at our school.
3 How many cars **have/has** your parents got?
4 We**'ve/'re** got a house, but unfortunately we **have/haven't** got a yard.
5 **Has got Mo/Has Mo got** any money?

Likes and dislikes

3 **Look at the questionnaire about students' preferences for school subjects and write sentences about the information.**

	😁	🙂	😐	😫
Scott	P.E.		math	geography
Rhiannon	math	geography	P.E.	
Libby	P.E.	geography	math	

1 Scott and Libby / P.E.
2 Rhiannon / math
3 Rhiannon and Libby / geography
4 Libby and Scott / study math
5 Rhiannon / do P.E.
6 Scott / geography

Question words

4 **Complete the interview with question words.**

Interviewer: Excuse me. **1** _________ languages do you speak?
David: Two. I speak Welsh and English.
Interviewer: Really? **2** _________ do you speak Welsh?
David: Because my parents are from Wales.
Interviewer: **3** _________ language do you speak at home?
David: We speak Welsh.
Interviewer: And **4** _________ do you speak Welsh with, apart from your parents?
David: I speak it with friends in other countries, on Skype.
Interviewer: In other countries? **5** _________ do people speak Welsh?
David: In the UK, Canada, Argentina and Australia.
Interviewer: Interesting! **6** _________ do you say 'thank you' in Welsh?
David: Diolch.
Interviewer: Well, diolch, and bye!

there is/are

5 **Write sentences with *there is/isn't* and *there are/aren't*.**

1 30 students in our class **(+)**
There are 30 students in our class.
2 a gym at the school **(–)**
3 a cafeteria **(+)**
4 a school uniform **(–)**
5 whiteboards in all the classrooms **(+)**
6 a lot of rules **(–)**

6 **Write questions about the picture.**

1 How many / movie theaters ?
2 a shopping center ?
3 any bike lanes ?
4 How many / subway stations ?
5 a library ?
6 What / near the sports center ?
7 any restaurants ?

7 **Answer the questions in exercise 6.**

1 *There are two movie theaters.*

Object pronouns

8 **Replace the words in bold with object pronouns.**

1 Can you come here, Jo? I want to see **Jo**.
Can you come here, Jo? I want to see you.
2 Where are my books? I can't find **my books**.
3 When you see Mom, can you ask **Mom** to call?
4 My sister and I often visit my cousins, but they don't visit **my sister and me**.
5 My favorite subject is math. I love **math**!
6 My uncle lives in Australia. I don't see **my uncle** very often.

Unit 1

Simple present

1 Reinforcement **Complete the sentences with the simple present form of the verbs in parentheses.**

1 I ________ **(not spend)** nine hours a day in front of a screen!
2 My dad ________ **(enjoy)** watching cooking shows.
3 My brother ________ **(not watch)** TV. He ________ **(watch)** movies on his computer.
4 One of my friends ________ **(follow)** a lot of YouTubers.
5 We ________ **(play)** video games on the weekend, but we ________ **(not play)** on school days.
6 My sister ________ **(go)** to the movie theater, but I ________ **(prefer)** to watch a series on Netflix.

2 Reinforcement **Order the words to make questions.**

1 you / upload videos to the Internet / do ?
2 do / you / how much time / online / spend ?
3 your friend / does / to your house / come / to play video games ?
4 where / you / do / watch TV ?
5 your teacher / does / how often / show a video in class ?

3 Reinforcement **Answer the questions in exercise 2.**

4 Challenge **Complete the article with the simple present form of the verbs in the box.**

add build go make not show not use take watch

Morgan Spence, from Glasgow in Scotland, is a young movie-maker. He **1** ________ to school during the day and **2** ________ movies in his free time. The interesting thing about his movies is that he **3** ________ real actors. He creates movies using LEGO.

Morgan **4** ________ scenes from famous movies in LEGO. Then he **5** ________ photos of the scenes and puts them together using a technique called Stop Motion. He **6** ________ the original music and dialogue from the movies later.

They **7** ________ his movies at the movie theater, but you can see them online. Millions of his followers **8** ________ them!

5 Challenge **Write questions about the course.**

LDC ACADEMY | COURSES | ADMISSIONS | NEWS & EVENTS

Movie-making course for 13- to 17-year-olds
April 4th–15th
Learn to use a camera. Write and make your own movie. Show it in the Academy's movie theater.

1 When / the course / start ?
____
2 When / it / finish ?
____
3 How old / you / need / to be ?
____
4 you / learn / to make a movie ?
____
5 the academy / show / the movies in a real movie theater ?
____

6 Challenge **Answer the questions in exercise 5. Use full sentences.**

Adverbs and expressions of frequency

7 Reinforcement **Rewrite the sentences with the adverbs and expressions of frequency in parentheses.**

1 My friends and I play role-playing games. **(often)**
2 My parents go to the movies. **(once a month)**
3 We watch TV these days. **(hardly ever)**
4 I use apps on my phone. **(every day)**
5 My brother is in front of his computer! **(always)**

8 Challenge **Complete the second sentence with an adverb or expression of frequency. Use the words in the box to help you.**

always every hardly ever never once twice

1 Tom watches his favorite series on Mondays and Thursdays. He ...
2 Joe plays video games seven days a week. He ...
3 Katy doesn't use social media much. She ...
4 Tony uploads a new video on Fridays. He ...
5 Edi is in front of her computer all the time. She ...
6 Ali hates horror movies. She ...

Simple present and present progressive

9 Reinforcement **Circle the correct option.**

1 My friends **don't read/aren't reading** every day.
2 Right now, we **study/'re studying** a play.
3 What **do you listen/are you listening** to? It sounds terrible!
4 My mom **usually borrows/is usually borrowing** books from the library.
5 We **have/'re having** a book exchange once a month at my school.

10 Challenge **Complete the blog with the simple present or present progressive form of the verbs.**

Hi, Sarah Dukes here. Today, I **1** _______________ (**write**) to you from Book Con. **2** _______________ (**you / know**) Comic Con®? Well, it's like that, but it's for fans of books. It **3** _______________ (**take**) place every year in New York, and some of the most important writers **4** _______________ (**come**) here. It **5** _______________ (**have**) workshops for young authors too.

Right now, people **6** _______________ (**wait**) to go in. They **7** _______________ (**not / wear**) costumes (OK, so it's not exactly like Comic Con), but they're very excited. Book Con **8** _______________ (**not / happen**) in other cities, but maybe it will in the future.

Unit 2

(*there*) *was/were*, *could* and past time expressions

1 Reinforcement **Rewrite the sentences with (*there*) *was/wasn't* or *could*.**

1 There was a Roman city near here. **(-)**
There wasn't a Roman city near here.
2 The Mayan museum was in the city center. **(-)**
____
3 The Greeks were good at engineering. **(?)**
____
4 The Egyptians weren't the inventors of clocks. **(+)**
____
5 Carthage wasn't in Egypt. **(? where)**
____
6 We could see the exhibit about the Romans. **(-)**
____
7 The Aztecs couldn't speak Spanish. **(?)**
____

2 Reinforcement **Complete the sentences with the missing words.**

1 They were here ten minutes ________ .
2 She was born ________ 2009.
3 We couldn't go to the party ________ night.
4 I wasn't in class the day ________ yesterday.
5 I could swim ________ I was four years old.

3 Challenge **Look at Casper's notes and complete the sentences about the trip.**

choose what to visit ✓
worksheet to complete ✓
go around with friends ✓
leave building ✗
exhibit about Aztecs ✗
exhibit about Romans ground floor ✓

1 We ________ choose what to see.
2 There ________ a worksheet to complete during the visit.
3 We ________ go around with our friends.
4 We ________ leave the building.
5 There ________ any exhibits about the Aztecs.
6 The exhibit about the Romans ________ on the ground floor.

4 Challenge **Today is Monday, November 14, 2022. Use past time expressions to describe the dates.**

1 Sunday, November 13, 2022 *Yesterday*
2 Saturday, November 12, 2022
3 Monday, November 7– Friday, November 11, 2022
4 2021
5 October 17–21, 2022
6 Monday, November 7, 2022

Simple past

5 Reinforcement **Write the simple past form of the verbs in the box. Which verb is regular?**

be can come do get go have
live read see speak think write

6 Challenge **Write a question for each answer. Use the ideas in the box to help you.**

a bike a shower at home
at your house homework in class
milk speak English swim TV

1 Yes, I did.
Did you do your homework last night?
2 Yes, I could.
3 No, they weren't.
4 Yes, I was.
5 No, they didn't.
6 Yes, I did.
7 No, he couldn't.

used to

7 Reinforcement **Circle the correct option.**

1 I **used to share/use to share** a room with my brother.
2 I didn't use to like rap but now I **do/don't**.
3 **Did you used live/Did you use to live** here?
4 Did you use to go to the beach on vacation? **No, I usen't/No, I didn't**.
5 **She used to use/She used to using** a camera, but now she takes photos with her phone.
6 He **didn't use to/didn't used to** have long hair.

8 Challenge **Look at the pictures of Conor's room now and when he was three. Write sentences with *used to* and *didn't use to*.**

A

B

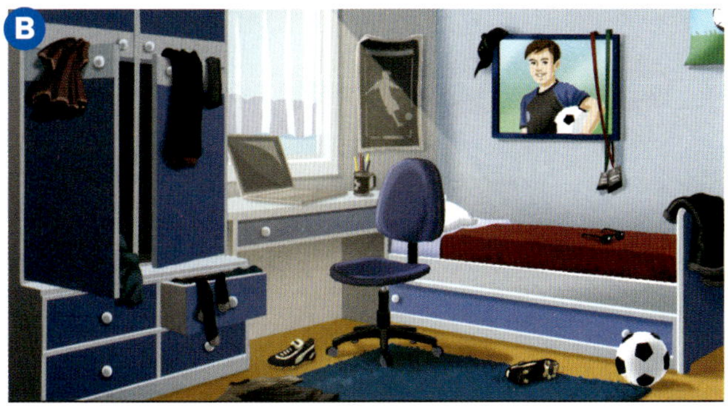

He used to like lots of different colors.

Unit 3

Past progressive

1 **Reinforcement** **Write affirmative and negative sentences with the past progressive.**

Yesterday, at 3:00 pm ...

1 Anna / play soccer **(skateboard)**

Anna wasn't playing soccer. She was ...

2 Tony / study Spanish **(play a video game)**

3 Sam and Clara / do their homework **(chat online)**

4 Louise / read **(watch a movie)**

5 Ben / write an email **(ride his bike)**

6 Geri, Sara and Pete / visit a museum **(shop)**

2 **Reinforcement** **Order the words to make questions.**

1 were / doing / what / you / yesterday at 3:00 pm ?
2 it / raining / was / two hours ago ?
3 watching TV / you / were / at ten o'clock last night ?
4 five minutes ago / the person next to you / was / doing / what ?
5 breakfast / you / having / were / seven thirty ?

3 **Reinforcement** **Answer the questions in exercise 2.**

4 **Challenge** **Look at the pictures and complete the sentences with the past progressive form of the verbs in the box.**

chat online get up go for a run have lunch make breakfast shop skateboard sleep watch a movie

1 At nine thirty, Taner ________________ .
2 At the same time, I ________________ .
3 At two o'clock, Lily and Greg ________________ .
4 At ten o'clock, Lily and Greg ________________ .
5 At ten o'clock, I ________________ .

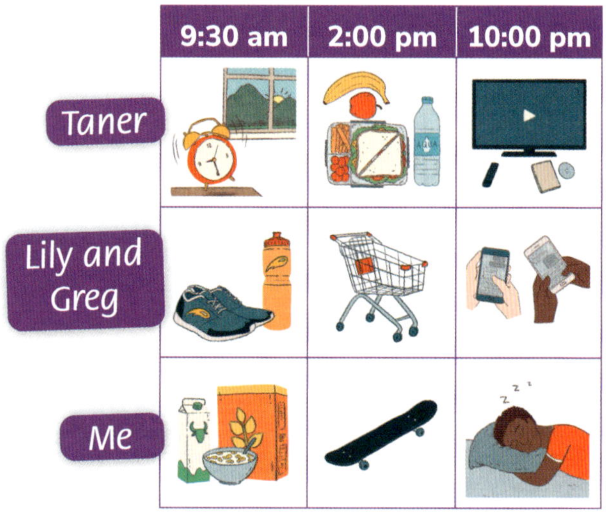

5 **Challenge** **Write questions about the activities in exercise 4.**

1 What / Lily and Greg / do / at nine thirty ?
2 Taner / play basketball / at two o'clock ?
3 What / you / do / at two o'clock ?
4 Taner / shop / at two o'clock ?
5 What / Taner / do / at ten o'clock ?

6 **Challenge** **Write answers to the questions in exercise 5.**

Simple past and past progressive

7 **Reinforcement** **Match 1–5 to a–e to make sentences.**

1 When you called, I was
2 I was finishing the test when
3 I fell asleep
4 We got lost while we
5 While I was cleaning

a were walking in the mountains.
b my room, I found my keys.
c while I was reading last night.
d the teacher told us to stop writing.
e practicing the guitar.

8 Challenge **Complete the story with the simple past or past progressive form of the verbs in parentheses.**

I can still remember when I **1** ________________ **(decide)** to join the robotics club. I **2** ________________ **(sit)** in the gym at the time. I **3** ________________ **(not feel)** very happy, but then I saw Toby the robot. It **4** ________________ **(run)** around the gym floor. A group of boys **5** ________________ **(use)** a remote control to move it and I **6** ________________ **(think)**, 'That looks fun!' The next day, I **7** ________________ **(join)** the club.

Six months later, I was on a plane. We **8** ________________ **(travel)** to our first robotics competition. We **9** ________________ **(not win)** the competition, but we **10** ________________ **(have)** a great time.

when and *while*

9 Reinforcement **Complete the sentences with *when* or *while*.**

1 We were playing a game ________ my dad called me.
2 My parents painted my room ________ I was staying with my cousin.
3 My brother broke his leg ________ he was skiing last winter.
4 We took lots of great photos ________ we were traveling around Italy.
5 My dad was using my computer ________ I got home from school yesterday.

10 Challenge **Write complete sentences in the simple past and past progressive with *when* or *while*.**

1 we / talk / outside school / the bell / ring **(when)**
____
2 my dad / work / I / get home yesterday **(when)**
____
3 someone / come / to the door / we / have / dinner last night **(while)**
____
4 I / try / sushi / for the first time / I / stay / with my cousins **(while)**
____
5 my brother / have / lunch in a café / someone / steal / his phone **(when)**
____

Unit 4

Quantifiers and (*not*) *enough*

1 Reinforcement **Match sentences 1–5 to pictures A–E.**

A __

B __

C __

D __

E __

1 There are some people.
2 There aren't any people.
3 There are too many people.
4 There aren't many people
5 There are a lot of people.

2 Reinforcement **Circle the correct option.**

1 It costs $20. You don't have **some/enough** money.
2 There were **too many/not many** people at the concert. I couldn't see a thing.
3 I don't have **some/any** time today, but I can help you tomorrow.
4 I had **too much/a lot of** fun at the party last night.
5 Is there **some/enough** food here for six?
6 I don't spend **much/some** money on clothes.

3 Challenge **Complete the sentences using the correct form of the words in the box.**

enough not any not many
some ~~too much~~ too many

1 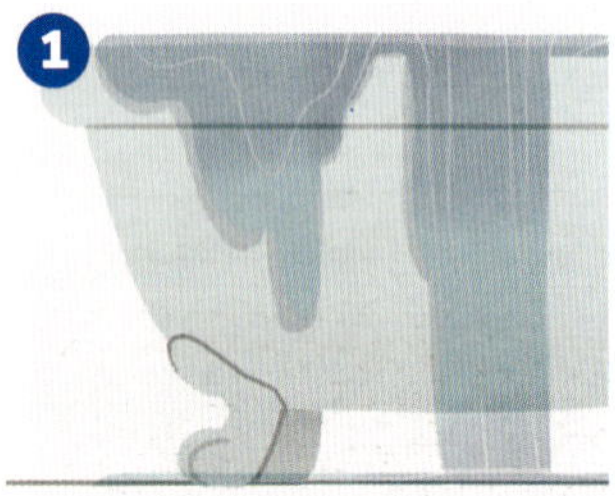

There *is too much* water in the bathtub.

2 

There ______________ food in fridge.

3 

There ______________ people in the elevator.

4 

There ______________ fruit in the bowl.

5 

There ______________ space in the suitcase.

6 

There ______________ chocolates in the box.

4 Challenge **Complete the sentences using a quantifier or *(not) enough*. Write one to five words in the blanks.**

1 The movie starts at 6:30. I live 30 minutes away and it's 6:15. I ______________ time.
2 We need 11 people for the soccer team. There are eight of us. There ______________ people.
3 There are no tomatoes in the store. They don't have ______________ tomatoes.
4 I have exercises for three subjects, an exam to study for, a presentation and 30 minutes free. I have ______________ homework.
5 He plays tennis and football and he bikes daily. He plays ______________ sports.

Comparatives, superlatives, *(not) as* + adjective + *as*

5 Reinforcement **Write the comparative and superlative of the adjectives in the box.**

bad big cheap expensive good happy
healthy important strong thin

6 Reinforcement **Read the information about three hotels. Are the sentences true or false? Write the answer in the blanks.**

	Seaview B & B	Sunny Days Resort	Paradise Hotel

Price	$100	$100	$180
Rooms	20	450	120
Year opened	1965	2019	2010
Food	★★	★	★★★★

1 Paradise is the cheapest. ______
2 Seaview is as expensive as Sunny Days. ______
3 Seaview is bigger than Paradise. ______
4 Sunny Days is the smallest hotel. ______
5 Paradise isn't as old as Seaview. ______
6 Sunny Days is the oldest. ______
7 The food at Sunny Days is better than the food at Seaview. ______
8 The food at Paradise is the worst. ______

7 Challenge **Complete the second sentence so it means the same as the first sentence.**

1 German is easier than Arabic. German isn't ...
2 Ireland isn't as big as England. Ireland is ...
3 Ohio is cheaper than New York. Ohio isn't ...
4 Soccer is less exciting than climbing. Soccer isn't ...
5 Madrid is smaller than Tokyo. Madrid isn't ...
6 Yoga and swimming are both equally healthy. Yoga is ...

8 Challenge **Look at the table in exercise 6. Write five new true sentences about the three hotels using comparatives, superlatives and *(not) as* + adjective + *as*.**

Sunny Days isn't as expensive as Paradise.

Unit 5

will for predictions: affirmative and negative

1 Reinforcement **Complete the sentences with *will*/*won't* and the verbs in the box.**

build   live   not have   not need   sleep

1 I think that we ________ in smaller houses in the future.
2 We ________ space to build big houses.
3 We ________ , cook and relax all in one room.
4 We ________ a lot of furniture for these homes.
5 Architects ________ them using recycled materials.

2 Challenge **Use the notes to write sentences about homes of the future. Use *will* and *won't*.**

Homes of the future

- control everything with voices
- people not go to work – work at home
- virtual wardrobes – tell us what to wear
- couch changes color depending on how we feel
- no problems sleeping – bed monitors how we sleep
- gardens not outside – plants and trees inside home

We'll control everything with our voices.

will for predictions: questions

3 Reinforcement **Complete the questions with the words in parentheses. Then match the questions to the answers.**

1 How ______________ in the future? **(shopping / change)**
2 ______________ or will students study at home? **(schools / exist)**
3 What languages ______________ ? **(people / speak)**
4 ______________ on virtual vacations? **(we / go)**

a I think people will buy more things online.
b Definitely! But I think people will travel too.
c We'll probably learn while we're sleeping!
d The same as now, but we'll have apps to translate.

4 Challenge **Write *Wh-* questions about the words in bold.**

1 **Robots** will help us by cleaning our houses.
____
2 **No**, we won't have flying cars.
____
3 People will live for **100 years**.
____
4 We will eat **the same as today, but less meat**.
____
5 People will go to **the moon** on vacation.
____

5 Challenge **Write your own answers to the questions in exercise 4.**

might

6 Reinforcement **Circle the correct option.**

1 I **won't/might** go to college, but it depends on my exam results.
2 I **won't/might** study engineering, because I'm not very good at math.
3 I don't want to live in another country, but I **might /will** spend a year overseas. I'm not sure.
4 My friends are very important to me, so I'm sure I **won't/will** always have the same friends.
5 I **will/won't** get married before I'm 30. I'd like to get a good job first.
6 I love fast cars, so who knows, I **won't/might** have a Porsche!

7 Challenge **Complete the text with *will*, *won't* or *might* and the ideas in the notes.**

Definitely not!	Maybe!	Definitely!
have a lot of children	start a company	travel
be a teacher	learn Japanese	play in a band

My future!

I'm not sure what job I'd like to do, but I don't like school, so I know I **1** ________ *! I'd like to be my own boss, so I* **2** ________ *– something to do with computers, that would be perfect. I want to visit other countries, so I'm sure I* **3** ________ *in the future. I'd love to go to Japan. I'd like to speak another language, so I* **4** ________ *. I'd like to get married, but I* **5** ________ *– just one or two. I hate sports, but I love music, so I won't play on a sports team, but I hope that I* **6** ________ *!*

First conditional

8 Reinforcement **Complete the sentences with the correct form of the verbs in parentheses.**

1 If we don't recycle, it ________________ **(be)** bad for the planet.
2 A lot of plastic will go into the oceans if we ________________ **(not recycle)** it.
3 We ________________ **(not have)** forests if we cut down all the trees.
4 Our air will be more polluted if our forests ________________ **(disappear)**.
5 If our air quality ________________ **(not improve)**, it will be dangerous for our health.

9 Challenge **Which sentences are correct? Correct the incorrect sentences.**

1 If we don't take care of the planet, it gets hotter.
2 If the climate will get hotter, the ice caps will melt.
3 If the ice caps melt, sea levels will go up.
4 Some cities disappear if the sea levels rise.
5 If cities are under water, people don't have homes.

Zero conditional

10 Reinforcement **Write sentences in the zero conditional. Use a comma where necessary.**

1 If / I / feel / cold / I / turn up / the heating
2 My mom / drive / me to school / if / I / be / late
3 If / my dad / not turn off / the computer / I / do it
4 I / recycle / things / if / my parents / forget
5 Tim / always / pick up / trash / if he / see it

11 Challenge **Complete the tips with the zero or first conditional of the verb in parentheses.**

HOW TO USE LESS PLASTIC

- Carry a reusable bag. Plastic bags **1** ________ **(take)** 1,000 years to degrade if you throw them away.
- Buy fresh food. If you **2** ________ **(not buy)** food covered in plastic, you **3** ________ **(not produce)** as much waste.
- Carry a reusable water bottle. Every plastic bottle **4** ________ **(go)** into the oceans or landfills if we **5** ________ **(not recycle)** it.
- If you use a paper bag for your packed lunch, it **6** ________ **(not take)** as long to degrade.
- If we **7** ________ **(not stop)** using plastic, soon there **8** ________ **(be)** more plastic in the oceans than fish!

Unit 6

Present perfect: affirmative and negative

1 Reinforcement **Look at the grid and find eight past participles.**

B	G	I	V	E	N
E	D	O	N	E	T
E	A	T	E	N	A
N	S	E	E	N	K
M	A	D	E	Q	E
W	F	L	O	W	N

2 Reinforcement **Order the words to make sentences.**

1 traveled / he / to three continents / has
____
2 haven't / under the stars / they / slept
____
3 three different houses / I've / lived / in
____
4 with dolphins / she / before / swum / hasn't
____
5 I've / three times / that book / read
____
6 met / haven't / before / we / them
____

3 Challenge **Write the base forms and simple past forms for the past participles.**

1 had 3 seen 5 swum
2 met 4 slept 6 written

4 Challenge **Are the sentences correct? Give reasons for your answers.**

1 I haven't been to this café before. It's nice.
2 Lulu isn't here. She's been to the gym.
3 I think I've gone here before. It looks familiar.
4 My uncle goes on very exciting vacations. He's gone to India, Canada and Australia.
5 He'll be back in five minutes. He's only gone to buy some bread.
6 Max isn't well so he's gone to the doctor's.

5 **Challenge** **Complete the text with the affirmative or negative present perfect form of the verbs in the box.**

be do eat find go have try visit

Sal Lavallo started traveling when he was 14 with a trip to China and Japan and now he has **1** ________________ **(+)** every country in the world! It **2** ________________ **(-)** easy: he **3** ________________ **(+)** some problems with visas and he **4** ________________ **(+)** to some countries we might think are dangerous, but he **5** ________________ **(-)** it difficult to make friends. He **6** ________________ **(+)** some strange things too: he **7** ________________ **(+)** goat's head in three countries and he **8** ________________ **(+)** a whole bat!

Present perfect: questions

6 **Reinforcement** **Rewrite the sentences with the words in parentheses.**

1 Have you flown a kite? **(ever)**
2 I've done a bungee jump. **(never)**
3 Has your brother ever laser tag? **(played)**
4 They've never a dance class before. **(taken)**
5 Have you and your friends acted in a play? **(ever)**
6 They never ridden a horse. **(have)**

7 **Challenge** **Look at the colors and make sentences in the present perfect. Use *ever*, *never* or nothing (0).**

you	they	ever/ never/0	design an app	meet a famous person
my friend	have/has	keep a diary	sing karaoke	do a bungee jump

1 (–) 
My friend has never designed an app.
2 (?)
3 (–)
4 (+)
5 (?)
6 (–)
7 (?)
8 (+)
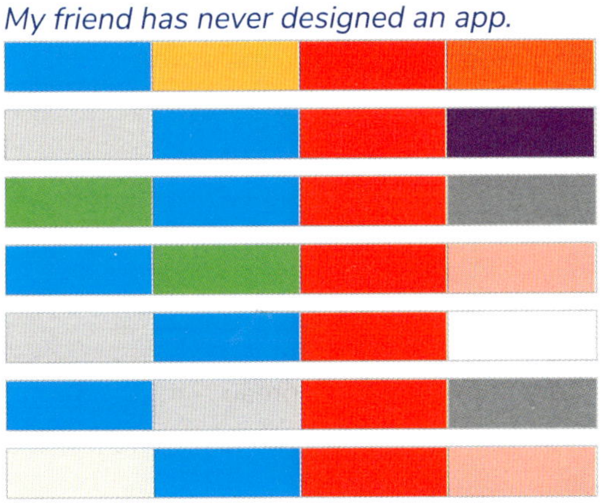

Unit 7

Present perfect with *for* and *since*

1 **Reinforcement** **Circle the correct option.**

1 **for/since** a week
2 **for/since** 2018
3 **for/since** January
4 **for/since** ten months
5 **for/since** a long time
6 **for/since** Monday
7 **for/since** five years
8 **for/since** I was born

2 **Reinforcement** **Write questions in the present perfect.**

1 How long / you / have / that silver watch ?
2 How long / you / be / a fan of Atlético Madrid ?
3 How long / your uncle / live / in Australia ?
4 How long / your parents / know / each other ?
5 How long / your sister / own / a car ?

3 **Reinforcement** **Complete the answers with *for* or *since*. Then match the answers with the questions in exercise 2.**

a I've liked them ________ I was five! __
b They met at school, so ________ 20 years. __
c ________ my last birthday. It was a present. __
d He's been there ________ 2010. He loves it! __
e Not long. She's had it ________ about a month. __

4 **Challenge** **Complete the description with the present perfect form of the verbs in parentheses and *for* or *since*.**

Jed and I **1** ________________ **(know)** each other **2** ________ a long time. In fact, we **3** ________________ **(live)** next door to each other **4** ________ we were born. He loves sports and he **5** ________________ **(be)** on an ice-hockey team **6** ________ six years. We used to play tennis too, but we **7** ________________ **(not play)** together **8** ________ March because he's always so busy.

5 **Challenge** **Write questions with *How long*?**

1 you / know / the person next to you
How long have you known the person next to you?
2 you / be / awake today
3 your teacher / live / here
4 you / have / the same hairstyle
5 you / like / your favorite singer
6 your parents / own / their car

6 Challenge **Answer the questions in exercise 5 with full sentences. Use the present perfect and *for* or *since*.**

I've known the person next to me ...

Present perfect and simple past

7 Reinforcement **Which two sentences are correct? Give reasons for your answers.**

1 I lived in Florida all my life. I love it here!
2 Where have you bought your new phone?
3 I didn't see a movie at the movie theater for a long time.
4 What did you do after school yesterday?
5 We haven't had a vacation last summer.
6 Jess has wanted to be a singer since she was five!
7 My mom worked in the same job since 2014.

8 Reinforcement **Correct the incorrect sentences in exercise 7.**

9 Challenge **Write sentences with the present perfect or simple past.**

1 We / have / a lot of exams / last week

2 He / wear / those sneakers / every day / for six months

3 She / not clean / her bedroom / yesterday

4 He / do / karate / since he was five

5 They / not / win / a game / for a long time

6 She / travel / to Paris / two years ago

Time expressions

10 Reinforcement **Complete the sentences with the time expressions in the box.**

ago all his life I was eight
last week six months

1 I've been a member of the gym for _________ .
2 My room isn't messy. I just cleaned it _________ .
3 I've had this game since _________ .
4 My sister started drama school two years _________ .
5 My grandpa has been a mechanic _________ .

11 Challenge **Rewrite the second sentence so that it means the same as the first sentence. Use no more than three words.**

1 I got a new tablet three weeks ago.
I've had my new tablet _______________ .
2 I've lived in this apartment since I was born.
I've lived in this apartment all _______________ .
3 I met Alex when I was ten.
I've known Alex _______________ ten.
4 Lucy has been on the hockey team for two years.
Lucy started playing on the hockey team _______________ .

Unit 8

have to

1 Reinforcement **Complete the sentences with the correct form of *have to*.**

1 Natalia *has to* (+) water the plants.
2 Angela and Alex _______________ (+) set the table.
3 Keira _______________ (–) take out the trash.
4 Ana and Charlie _______________ (+) to do the dishes.
5 _______________ (?) Oliver _______________ (?) take the dog for a walk?
6 I _______________ (–) to do the dusting.

2 Reinforcement **Look at the information about a school trip and write complete sentences.**

✓	✗
~~Sign up by Friday 22nd~~ Pay Mrs. Hebel by Tuesday 26th Arrive at 8:00 am Wear walking boots	Wear school uniform Bring school books Bring a packed lunch

You have to sign up by Friday 22nd.

3 Challenge **Look at the information in exercise 2. Write questions for the answers with *have to*.**

1 By Friday 22nd.
When do you have to sign up for the trip?
2 Mrs. Hebel.
3 8:00 am.
4 Yes, we have to wear walking boots.
5 Clothes for the mountains.
6 No, we don't. We're going to eat in the café there.

4 Challenge **Write six sentences about the household chores you have to and don't have to do. Use expressions in the list.**

clean the bathroom
dry the dishes
empty the dishwasher
hang out the laundry
take care of my brother or sister
take out the recycling
clean my room
water the plants
take the dog for a walk
feed the goldfish
sweep the floor
cut the grass

will and *going to*

5 Reinforcement **Put the missing word in the correct position in each sentence.**

1 OK, I'll you at 6 o'clock. **(meet)**
2 Yes, I'm going see him on Wednesday. **(to)**
3 I help you with your homework. **(will)**
4 My parents going to be away this weekend. **(are)**

6 Reinforcement **Match sentences a–d with sentences 1–4 from exercise 5 and decide which comes first in each pair to make short dialogues.**

a The movie starts at 6:15.
b Can your dad take us to practice on Saturday?
c I don't understand this exercise.
d Can anyone take this to Luke?

7 Challenge **Order the words to make sentences or questions.**

1 is / Eva / going / next month / get married / to
2 give / your / tomorrow / math book / I'll / you
3 going / you / What time / are / arrive / to ?
4 isn't / Mrs. Jones / to / going / tomorrow / be / at school

8 Challenge **Circle the correct option.**

1 I **will watch/'m going to** watch a handball game with my cousin on Friday.
2 It's very hot in here. I**'ll/'m going to** open the window.
3 I**'ll/'m going to** tell you tomorrow if I can come on Saturday.
4 Jay **will/is going to** study in Canada next year.
5 There isn't any milk but I spoke to Dad. He **will/is going to** buy some on the way home from work.
6 A: We don't have any milk.
B: OK. **I'll/I'm going to** buy some later.

Pronunciation

Unit 1

/s/ /z/ /ɪz/

For nouns and verbs finishing in *s*, *ss*, *sh*, *ch*, *x* or *z*, add an extra syllable /ɪz/.

1 49 **Listen to the plural nouns. Copy and complete the table with the words you hear.**

/s/ or /z/	/ɪz/
movies	*buses*

2 50 **Listen to the verbs. Copy and complete the table with the verbs you hear.**

/s/ or /z/	/ɪz/
speaks	*watches*

3 51 **Work in pairs. Find five words ending in /ɪz/. Listen and check, then repeat.**

actors boxes buys changes dances finishes gets offices talks umbrellas

Unit 2

/ʊ/ and /u/

1 52 **Listen to the pairs of words. Do they contain the same sound, or different sounds?**

1 book / food
2 cook / shoe
3 pool / school
4 could / good
5 rule / true
6 look / put

2 53 **Copy and complete the table with the words in exercise 1. Listen and check.**

/ʊ/	/u/
book	*food*

3 **Work in pairs. Practice saying the sentences. Pay attention to /ʊ/ and /u/.**

1 I'm a really good cook.
2 Your shoes are next to the pool.
3 Could I take a look at your book?
4 We have a lot of school rules.

Unit 3

Word linking

In sentences, a consonant sound often links to a vowel sound to help connect the words.

1 54 **Listen and repeat the sentences. Notice the consonant–vowel links.**

He's a doctor. She studies English. They live in America.

2 55 **Find the words which link in the sentences. Listen and repeat.**

1 She drives a car.
2 Do you have a pen?
3 It's five o'clock.
4 He's an artist.

3 56 **Listen and find seven examples of linking. Then practice saying the text.**

What is a good job? For me, it's not important to be rich, but I would like to be part of a team and feel that I make a difference.

Unit 4

Weak forms in comparatives

The pronunciation of *as* ... *as* is /əz/ ... /əz/. We pronounce *-er* endings in comparative adjectives /ər/. The pronunciation of *than* is /ðən/.

1 57 **Listen to the comparative adjectives.**

better bigger cheaper colder older taller

2 58 **Listen and repeat the sentences.**

1 My bag is bigger than yours.
2 Your English is better than mine.
3 This phone is cheaper than that one.

3 59 **Work in pairs. Listen and repeat the sentences. Pay attention to the /əz/, /ər/ and /ðən/ sounds.**

1 It's colder than yesterday.
2 Jamie isn't as tall as me.
3 English isn't as difficult as Chinese.
4 Football is more exciting than golf.

Unit 5

Diphthongs /eɪ/ /aɪ/ /oʊ/

Diphthongs are when you pronounce two individual sounds together, for example /e/ and /ɪ/ become /eɪ/.

1 60 **Listen and repeat the sounds.**

1 /eɪ/ day 2 /aɪ/ my 3 /oʊ/ go

2 61 **Copy and complete the table with the words in the box. Listen and check.**

~~bike~~ grow home light make night paper phone recycle ride save take throw waste

/eɪ/ day	/aɪ/ my	/oʊ/ go
	bike	

3 62 **Work in pairs. Practice saying the sentences. Pay attention to the diphthongs.**

1 Save the planet before it's too late!
2 Turn off lights at night.
3 Grow your own food at home.
4 Ride your bike every day.
5 Recycle paper and phones.

Unit 6

Consonant clusters

Some words are difficult to say because they have several consonants together.

1 63 **Listen and repeat the words. Which word doesn't have a consonant cluster at the end?**

broken climb plastic screen sport three

2 64 **Which words in the box do not have a consonant cluster at the end? Listen and repeat.**

dressed helped left milk shelf stop thanks

3 **Find the words with consonant clusters. Then practice saying the sentences.**

1 Chips are my favorite snack.
2 My friend's brother often camps in spring.
3 My cousins lived in the southwest of Spain.

Unit 7

for, since and sentence stress

1 65 **We normally pronounce *for* /fər/. Listen and repeat the phrases.**

for two minutes for five hours for ten days for two weeks for four years

2 66 **We pronounce *since* /sɪns/. Listen and repeat the phrases.**

since 2010 since I was born since June since ten o'clock since yesterday

3 67 **We usually stress information words. Listen and repeat the sentences.**

1 They've **lived** here since **September**.
2 I've **had** this **phone** for **six months**.

4 68 **Find the stressed words in the sentences. Then listen and check.**

1 She's been at this school since 2018.
2 He hasn't seen his grandmother for a long time.

Unit 8

have to

When we say *have to* in a sentence, it is usually unstressed. The pronunciation of *have to* is /hæftə/.

1 69 **Listen to the sentences. Notice the pronunciation of *have to*.**

1 I have to set the table.
2 I don't have to sweep the floor.

2 70 **Listen and repeat the sentences. Pay attention to the pronunciation of *have to*.**

1 I have to clean my room.
2 I don't have to make dinner.
3 We have to clear the table.
4 They don't have to water the plants.

3 **Work in pairs. Talk about things you have to or don't have to do at home. Remember to pronounce *have to* /hæftə/.**

clean my room clear the table
do the dishes make my bed
set the table take out the trash

Project planner

Unit 1 Graphic organizer

What makes a good story?

- Making your own stories
  - teens who make movies, music videos & video games
- Stories in movies, shows & games
  - strategy games, adventure games, sports games
  - thriller, drama series, comedy
- Talking about things you like and dislike
  - 'I'm (not) interested in …'
  - 'I'm (not) crazy about …'
- Writing a review
  - 'The story takes place in …'
  - 'I love this story because …'
- Talking about what you'd like to watch
  - 'Would you rather … ?' 'I don't mind.' 'I'd prefer.'

How to plan visual output

- **Organize your space** before you start. Use a ruler!
- Include an attractive **title** or heading.
- **Black and white** or **color**?
- **Do a rough plan** before you begin.

Unit 2 Graphic organizer

What can we learn from history?

- How the Aztecs changed the world
  - farms on water
  - two calendars
- Everyday objects in the past
  - alarm clock, comb
  - scissors, change purse
- Stages of life
  - be born, get married, retire
- School life in Ancient Egypt
  - students used paper
  - girls didn't go to school
- First Nations people
  - people used to learn Haida
- An email about life in the past and now
  - 'We used to play soccer.'
  - 'I went to the local school.'

How to present to an audience

- Make **eye contact**.
- **Don't block the presentation** with your body.
- Use **gestures** to keep attention.
- **Point** to things in your presentation as you speak.
- **Don't speak too fast** – people need time to understand.
- Remember to **smile**!

Unit 3 Graphic organizer

- **What is your idea of success?**
  - Success in business
    - overcoming difficulties
    - the history of 3 successful companies
  - Personal success
    - win a prize, get good grades, make a difference
  - Word families related to success
    - achieve - achievement
    - invent - invention
    - compete - competition
  - Success stories
    - Afghan girls in robotics competition

How to give a visual presentation

- Introduce a section, then **give people time to read**.
- Don't just read the infographic aloud. **Give additional information**.
- **Explain** what the photos and images show.
- **Don't go too fast**. People need to time to listen and understand.

Unit 4 Graphic organizer

- **How can teenagers learn about money?**
  - Comparing things
    - 'It isn't as expensive as …'
    - 'It's the easiest way'
  - Money words
    - discount
    - earn
    - sell
  - Money for your old things
    - LEGO
    - old phones
    - Happy Meal toys
  - The Money Quiz
    - Are you good with money?
  - New-style Stores
    - less traditional stores
  - Giving advice about money
    - 'Why don't you … ?'
    - 'You should …'

How to create a digital presentation

- Make a **different slide for each idea**.
- **Write key facts** on each slide.
- **Use short sentences.**
- **Ask questions.**
- **Use a picture** for each slide – make this funny, beautiful, relevant.
- Make sure you can **read the writing easily** (not blue text on blue background, or text on a picture).
- Use colors.

Unit 5 Graphic organizer

How can we improve our environment?

- Using new technologies
  - 3D printing of houses
  - recycling materials
- Describing where we live
  - hall, kitchen, stairs, armchair, cupboard, trash can
- Protecting the environment & resources
  - recycle waste, reuse things, plant trees …
  - phrasal verbs: turn off, cut down, pick up
- Planning a party without waste
  - 'What do you think about … ?' 'The good thing is …'
- People taking action
  - young campaigners: Feliz Finkbeiner, Nadia Sparkes
  - family living plastic-free

How to present arguments

- Make a **limited number** of points.
- Support each point with one or more **examples**.
- Indicate clearly when you are **starting a new section**.
- **Summarize** the main points again at the end.

Unit 6 Graphic organizer

Why might it be a good idea to try new things?

- Experience gift ideas
  - a DJ session, a masterclass, a recording studio session
- Collocations: experiences
  - go zip lining, sing karaoke, swim with dolphins
- Jenk Oz
  - he's acted in a play, he's met Adele, he's been go-karting
  - iCoolkid – a guide to all things cool to see and do
- Describing experiences
  - 'We've ridden horses.'
  - 'We've slept under the stars.'
- Talking about experience in an interview

How to create a meme

- Use **a free online meme generator**.
- Upload **a photo** or look for a photo in the meme library.
- Write your **meme statement**. Make it short!
- Click **save**.
- **Copy** your meme to your document.
- Make sure you give your document a **heading**.

Unit 7 Graphic organizer

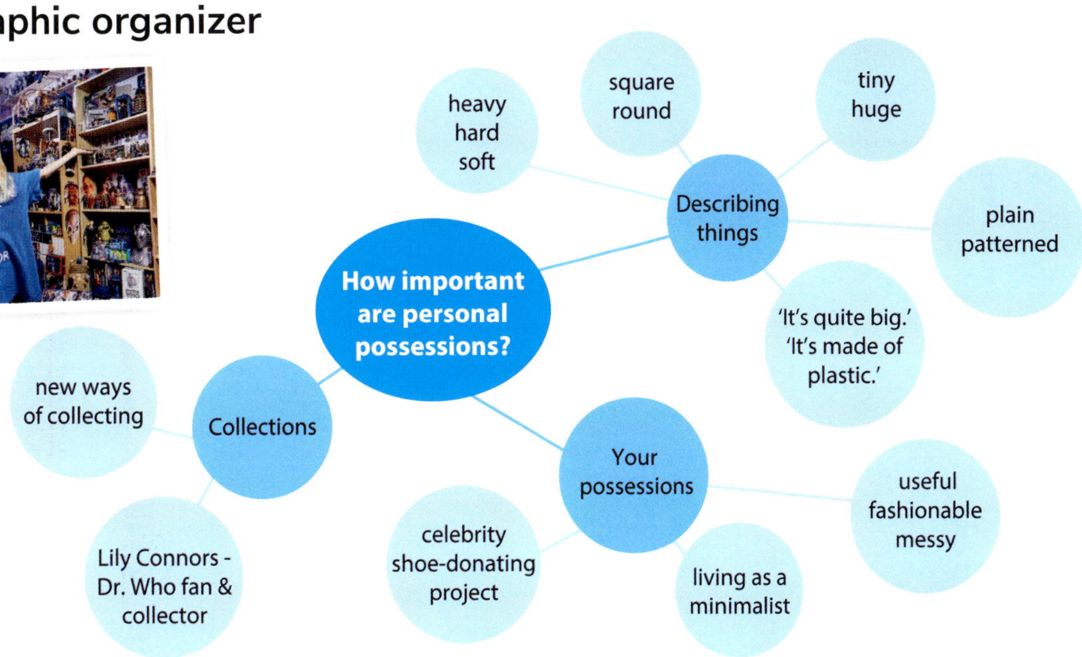

How to make a video

- **Practice** before you film.
- **Ask someone** to film you or **do it yourself**.
- Take a **general shot** and then **focus on some items** as you describe them.
- **Speak slowly** and clearly.
- Remember: if you aren't happy, you can always **do it again**.

Unit 8 Graphic organizer

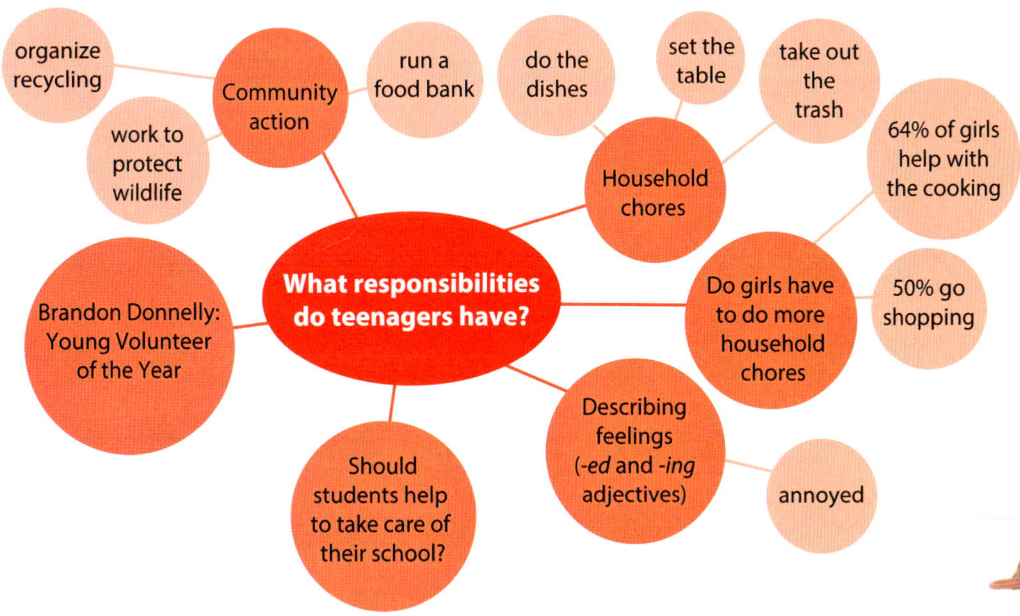

How to present ideas

- Decide on the **format** to display your proposal (poster, digital presentation etc.).
- **Plan** your presentation. Have you answered all the questions?
- Use **short sentences** on your poster or slides and include more detail when you present.
- Speak clearly and don't forget to use **gestures**.

Irregular verbs

Base form	Simple past	Past participle
be /bi/	**was/were** /wɑz/ /wɜr/	**been** /bɪn/
become /bɪ'kʌm/	**became** /bɪ'keɪm/	**become** /bɪ'kʌm/
begin /bɪ'gɪn/	**began** /bɪ'gæn/	**begun** /bɪ'gʌn/
break /breɪk/	**broke** /broʊk/	**broken** /'broʊkən/
bring /brɪŋ/	**brought** /brɔt/	**brought** /brɔt/
build /bɪld/	**built** /bɪlt/	**built** /bɪlt/
buy /baɪ/	**bought** /bɔt/	**bought** /bɔt/
catch /kætʃ/	**caught** /kɔt/	**caught** /kɔt/
choose /tʃuz/	**chose** /tʃoʊz/	**chosen** /'tʃoʊz(ə)n/
come /kʌm/	**came** /keɪm/	**come** /kʌm/
cut /kʌt/	**cut** /kʌt/	**cut** /kʌt/
do /du/	**did** /dɪd/	**done** /dʌn/
drink /drɪŋk/	**drank** /dræŋk/	**drunk** /drʌŋk/
drive /draɪv/	**drove** /droʊv/	**driven** /'drɪv(ə)n/
eat /it/	**ate** /eɪt/	**eaten** /'it(ə)n/
fall /fɔl/	**fell** /fel/	**fallen** /'fɔlən/
feed /fid/	**fed** /fed/	**fed** /fed/
feel /fil/	**felt** /felt/	**felt** /felt/
find /faɪnd/	**found** /faʊnd/	**found** /faʊnd/
fly /flaɪ/	**flew** /flu/	**flown** /floʊn/
forget /fər'get/	**forgot** /fər'gɑt/	**forgotten** /fər'gɑt(ə)n/
get /get/	**got** /gɑt/	**got, gotten** /gɑt/ /'gɑt(ə)n/
give /gɪv/	**gave** /geɪv/	**given** /'gɪv(ə)n/
go /goʊ/	**went** /went/	**gone** /gɑn/
grow /groʊ/	**grew** /gru/	**grown** /groʊn/
hang /hæŋ/	**hung** /hʌŋ/	**hung** /hʌŋ/
have /hæv/	**had** /hæd/	**had** /hæd/
hear /hɪr/	**heard** /hɜrd/	**heard** /hɜrd/
hit /hɪt/	**hit** /hɪt/	**hit** /hɪt/

Base form	Simple past	Past participle
keep /kip/	**kept** /kept/	**kept** /kept/
know /noʊ/	**knew** /nu/	**known** /noʊn/
lay /leɪ/	**laid** /leɪd/	**laid** /leɪd/
leave /liv/	**left** /left/	**left** /left/
let /let/	**let** /let/	**let** /let/
lose /luz/	**lost** /lɑst/	**lost** /lɑst/
make /meɪk/	**made** /meɪd/	**made** /meɪd/
meet /mit/	**met** /met/	**met** /met/
pay /peɪ/	**paid** /peɪd/	**paid** /peɪd/
put /pʊt/	**put** /pʊt/	**put** /pʊt/
read /rid/	**read** /red/	**read** /red/
ride /raɪd/	**rode** /roʊd/	**ridden** /'rɪd(ə)n/
ring /rɪŋ/	**rang** /ræŋ/	**rung** /rʌŋ/
run /rʌn/	**ran** /ræn/	**run** /rʌn/
say /seɪ/	**said** /sed/	**said** /sed/
see /si/	**saw** /sɔ/	**seen** /sin/
sell /sel/	**sold** /soʊld/	**sold** /soʊld/
send /send/	**sent** /sent/	**sent** /sent/
shine /ʃaɪn/	**shone** /ʃoʊn/	**shone** /ʃoʊn/
sing /sɪŋ/	**sang** /sæŋ/	**sung** /sʌŋ/
sit /sɪt/	**sat** /sæt/	**sat** /sæt/
sleep /slip/	**slept** /slept/	**slept** /slept/
speak /spik/	**spoke** /spoʊk/	**spoken** /'spoʊkən/
spend /spend/	**spent** /spent/	**spent** /spent/
sweep /swip/	**swept** /swept/	**swept** /swept/
swim /swɪm/	**swam** /swæm/	**swum** /swʌm/
take /teɪk/	**took** /tʊk/	**taken** /'teɪkən/
teach /titʃ/	**taught** /tɔt/	**taught** /tɔt/
tell /tel/	**told** /toʊld/	**told** /toʊld/
think /θɪŋk/	**thought** /θɔt/	**thought** /θɔt/
throw /θroʊ/	**threw** /θru/	**thrown** /θroʊn/
understand /ˌʌndər'stænd/	**understood** /ˌʌndər'stʊd/	**understood** /ˌʌndər'stʊd/
wake /weɪk/	**woke** /woʊk/	**woken** /'woʊkən/
win /wɪn/	**won** /wʌn/	**won** /wʌn/
write /raɪt/	**wrote** /roʊt/	**written** /'rɪt(ə)n/

Macmillan Education Limited
4 Crinan Street
London N1 9XW

Companies and representatives throughout the world

Get Involved! American Edition Level 2 Student's Book ISBN 978-1-380-03319-2
Get Involved! American Edition Level 2 Student's Book with Student's App and Digital Student's Book ISBN 978-1-380-07218-4

First published 2022

Original design by Designers Educational Ltd and emc design ltd
Page make-up by Wild Apple Design Ltd and Composure
Illustrated by Alexandra Barboza (Lemonade Illustration Agency) pp. 121, 122; Esther Cuadrado (Beehive Illustration) pp. 89, 116; Daniela Geremia (Beehive Illustration) p. 119; Clive Goodyear (Beehive Illustration) p. 61; Tamara Joubert (Beehive Illustration) pp. 23, 25, 40; Camille Medina (Beehive Illustration) p. 120; Kate Sheppard (Beehive Illustration) p. 28; Joe Wilkins (Beehive Illustration) p. 117
Cover design by Designers Educational Ltd
Cover photographs by Getty Images/Marc Romanelli (tl), Getty images/martinedoucet (tr), Getty Images/Roderick Chen(cm), Getty Images/Tom Werner (bl), Getty Images/Roos Koole (br)
Picture research by Catherine Dunn
Cover picture research by Penelope Bowden, Proudfoot Pictures

Authors' acknowledgements
Gill would like to thank her friends from International House, Barcelona.
Kate would like to thank all her colleagues and friends at International House, Madrid.

The publishers would like to thank Nancy Contreras Guerrero; Luciana Gugliada S.; Nuria Julieta Holguin Añoveros, Colegio Benavente; Edith Dolores Islas Cabrera, Colegio Hispano Americano; Silvana Flores López, Instituto D'Amicis, S.C.; Monica Muñoz Castanón; Jaqueline Suzanne Torres Contreras.

The authors and publishers would like to thank the following for permission to reproduce their photographs:
From the Alamy Stock Photo collection Stock Photo pp. 87(bl), Classic Image pp. 24(tr), 25(H), Cultural Archive p. 25(G), George Fairbairn p. 51(bl), Jim Gibson p. 31(tr), Granger Historical Picture Archive p. 25(K), Robert Kawka pp. 11(2), 24(B, E), Jakub Krechowicz p. 95(baby sock), Lanmas p. 27(tr), Olekcii Mach p. 35(Tamagotchi), Matthew Leane p. 12(Star Wars), opturadesign p. 13(cl), Amilcar Pereira p. 51(background, b), Photo 12 pp. 12, 15, 19(Monster House), 130, Jozef Polc p. 90, Jeff Saunders Travel Stock p. 52, Alex Segre pp. 2, Bettina Strenske pp. 48(cl) 108(3), Bill Truran p. 51(cereal), Universal Images Group North America LLC p. 86(tc), WENN Rights Ltd pp. 51(tr), 131, World History Archive pp. 25(L), 108(5); Example of Canadian Haida art © **Alvin Child** p. 29(B); **Aquaflow Distributors** p. 68(4); **BBC** Studios Distribution Ltd p. 13(br), 61(br); **Biblioburro**/Louis Soriano p. 18; **Blend Images** pp. 14(tl), 108(8); **Corbis RF** pp. 41(trophy), 95(goggles); **www.cryptokitties.co** pp. 87(cr), 133; **E+** p. 38(camera); **DLA** p. 25(br); **Eyevine**/Matt Writtle pp. 11(6), 75(tr); © **First Nations Snowboarding Association** p. 29(D), 130(br); **Flickr** p. 86(tl); **Renata Flores** pp. 78, 132; fullmoonphoto.ca p. 29(c); **Getty Images** pp. 7(tr), 35(computer), 41(mountains), 59(slide 1), 60(background), 87(bl), 95(kiwi), 123ducu p. 75(inset), 26ISO pp. 15(bl), 131, Getty5m3photos p. 14(ctl), alexdimitrov p. 62(chairs), Anutik p. 77(recording), xabier arnau pp. 104(t), 106-107(background), Eric Audras p. 96(clear table), Jose Manuel Espinola Aguayo p. 61(H), annoying. orange p. 36(post-its), Arsela p. 92(C), BananaStock pp. 97(fish), 127(fish), Hoxton/Martin Barraud p. 15(cl), Axelle/Bauer-Griffin/Contributor p. 73(cr), bbostjan p. 44(trb), Alistair Berg pp. 37(6), Bet_Noire p. 60(A), Blend Images p. 20(t), Blend Images/Kidstock p. 14(cl), Evgenii_Bobrov p. 28, bonchan p. 96(dishwasher), Michael Barrett Boesen p. 9(trc), ol de Zuasnabar Brebbia p. 104(br), 107(background), Caiaimage p. 32(background), Vince Caligiuri pp. 11(9), 47(tr, br), Leonello Calvetti p. 72(4), Krissia Campos p. 86(tr), M.Cantarero p. 31(tr), Tsaiyun Chuang p. 80(background), chrupka p. 35(language map), cinoby p. 9(cr), Jean-Pierre Clatot p. 30, Carlos Clarivan p. 45(br), Matt Comeskey p. 83(tr), Comstock p. 26(c), Jeffrey Coolidge p. 91(mobile), Andy Crawford p. 35(Game Boy), d3sign/Moment p. 2(br), Daisy-Daisy p. 97(recycling), ddukang p. 60(D), Daniel Hurst Photography pp. 36(1), 131, danielvfung p. 15(cl), Davies and Starr p. 26(lr, tlb), Peter Dazeley pp. 36-37(background), 36(1), 131, De Agostini/G. Dagli Orti p. 25(J, K), Steve Debenport p. 108(2), © by Martin Deja p. 108(9), Danita Delimont pp. 11(5), 54(br), Devonyu p. 36(3), Digital Vision pp. 48(clothes), 131, Kristin Duvall pp. 95(notepad), 97(washing up), Tatiana Dyuvbanova pp. 61(J), 108(6), Rafa Elias p. 114(tr), Enot-poloskun p. 48(background, b), ewg3D p. 122(hotel), 73(12), fstop123 p. 99(washing up), Nicola Ferrara p. 75(bl), Filo p. 9(tr), Fiona1 pp. 97(sweep), 127(sweep), Fotsearch RF p. 96(lay table), Stephen Frink p. 73(13), Rich Fury p. 76, Gotham/Contributor p. 98, Granefelt, Lena p. 73(10), Steve Granitz/Contributor p. 87(bl), Grassetto p. 92(A), Maxim Grigoryev p. 63(tr), Axelle/Bauer-Griffin/Contributor p. 38(br), Daniel Grill p. 35(cassette), Antonio Guillem p. 97(dusting), Bartosz Hadyniak p. 99 (washing up), hadynyah pp. 99(b), 133, Tim Hall p. 85(tl), Laurent Hamels p. 61(I), Frazer Harrison/Staff p. 34(br), Eric Hernandez p. 61(K), Hero Images pp. 6(cl), 59(slide 5), 72(8), 77(tr), 83(tl), Hill Street Studios p. 72(5), Dave J Hogan/Contributor p. 50, Ian Hooton/SPL p. 73(11), Samir Hussein p. 42, Image Source pp. 61(M), 72(7), incomible p. 115(speech cloud), Erik Isakson p. 96(hang washing), istockphotos pp. 26(tl), 35(Nintendo), 36-37(frame), 38(mobile), 53(guitar), 59(slide 6), 91(pencil case), iStockphoto/ewg3D p. 6(br), istock/Grafner p. 115(popcorn), izusek p. 74(stage), Brian A Jackson pp. 97(mower), 127(mower), JazzIRT p. 60(C), A. Jemolo p. 24(D, F), Jovanmandic pp. 73(9), 133, Jonathan Knowles p. 53(baking), Ishii Koji p. 100, Bogdan Kurylo p. 66(br), kurga p. 38(trainers), LightFieldStudios p. 16, Lilkin p. 115(trainers), David Livingston/Stringer p. 17(br), John Lamb p. 109, VALERIE MACON p. 112(tl), Jovo Marjanovic p. 59(slide 3), DEA/L. De Masi p. 24(C), Peter Mason p. 77(DJ), Pam McLean p. 72(6), MentalArt p. 115(balloons), Jasmin Merdan pp. 2, 83(cr), miljko p. 103(tr), Mima Foto p. 48(euros), Mims p. 6(bl), MissHibiscus p. 99(tr), mofles pp. 27(br), 130(bl), Moment/Manuel Breva Colmeiro p. 12(background), monticelllo p. 115(clock), Amir Mukhtar p. 74(baking), mustafagull pp. 97(dog), 127(dog), Francois Nel p. 112(tr), Nora Carol Photography pp. 55(tr), Kasipat Phonlamai p. 71, photomanx21 p. 60(B), Pixeliebe p. 7(emojis), relif p. 37(5), rippinlines p. 72(background, 1), Tanya Rozhnovskaya p. 91(scarf), Kittipong Ruangroj p. 55(tr), RyanJLane p. 35(shell suit), Inti St Clair pp. 84, 97(mowing), Paolo De Santis pp. 60(E), SawitreeLyaon p. 96(rubbish), sbayram p. 68(background), Science Photo Library p. 92(B), Alan Shortall p. 108(7), Tom Sibley p. 108(4), skynesher p. 59(slide 4), Solstock p. 97(drying dishes), Henrik Sorensen p. 77(music), Squaredpixels p. 32(cr), Sascha Steinbach p. 65(trr), Studio p. 61(G), Michael Svoboda p. 44(tr), svetikd p. 62(tl), GAlex Treadway p. 74(bungee), Trutschel p. 59(slide 2), Betsie Van der Meer p. 73(14), VCG p. 63(bl), Klaus Vedfelt p. 17(tr), by Vesi_127 p. 96(put on washing), VisualCommunications p. 72(3), vladru pp. 61(L), 132, Scott Wallace p. 99(collecting wood), Andrew Bret Wallis p. 89, Westend61 pp. 44(background), 53(gardening), 63(br), 96(ironing), Kevin Winter/Staff p. 62(br), Ray Wise p. 6(mr), Wivoca p. 123, Marilyn Angel Wynn p. 29(A), yayayoyo pp. 15(cb), 60(F), ZargonDesign p. 41(podium), Zero Creatives p. 73(15), Zoa-Arts p. 48(girl and jar); **Gilaxia** pp. 2, 83(trc); Divergent cover - Reprinted by permission of **HarperCollins Publishers Ltd**, © Veronica Roth p. 20; **Instagram** p. 39(Instagram logo, Instagram screen shot); **Istockphoto** pp. 12(br), 91(sunglasses); © **Collection and Archive of Museum of Kotsanas Museum of Ancient Greek Technology** (www.kotsanas.com) pp. 11(2), 24(A); **Macmillan Education Limited** pp. 19(tl), 22, 31(tl), 34(cl), 37(br), 43(tl), 46, 49, 55(tl), 58, 67, 70, 73(br), 79, 82, 85(br), 91(tl, backpack), 97(br), 103(tl), p. 106, 115(notes), Haddon Davis p. 37(diary); **Zachary Maxwell** p. 115(tl); **Museum and Science Centre Luuppi** from Kierikinkangas Stone Age Dwelling site, Finland/Sami Viljanmaa p. 25(I); **Peek Project**/Brandon Donnelly pp. 11(3), 102; **Photodisc** pp. 92(background), 97(watering), 127(watering); **Plant-for-the-Planet** p. 65(trl); © **Polaroid** p. 39(Polaroid logo, Polaroid camera); **Shutterstock.com**/279photo Studio pp. 48(tl), Disney Studios/Kobal p. 19(Aladdin), Iakov Filimonov p. 73(16), David Fisher p. 47(bl), Ivan Garcia p. 36(2), Granger p. 27(cr), Frank Micelotta p. 13(tl), Ondacaracola p. 68(3), Adam Radosavljevic p. 68(1), Jim Lo Scalzo pp. 11(1), 41(r), 131, Narendra Shrestha p. 43(tr), null Marvel/Disney/Kobal p. 19(The Avengers), Photographee.eu p. 96(load dishwasher), Sony p. 19(MIB), Sony/Kobal p. 108(1), Universal/Kobal p. 19(Mamma Mia), Warner Bros/Toho/Kobal pp. 19(Toy Story), Warner Bros/DC/Kobal p. 114; **SWNS**/Melissa May p. 10(br), SWNS/Miles Soloman p. 44(br); **Thinkstock** pp. 72(2), 87(bl); **Andrew Twort** p. 68(2); Courtesy of **Vans** p. 39(VANS logo, cr); **Wales News Service**/Lily Conner pp. 88, 133.

Video footage and stills supplied by:
BBC Studios Distribution Ltd pp. 13, 61; Digeo Productions pp. 37, 73, 85, 97; DLA pp. 25, 49; MTJ pp. 19, 31, 43, 55, 67, 79, 91, 103; Maia Films pp. 22, 34, 46, 58, 70, 82, 94, 106.

Additional sources:
Spoors, Nick (12/30/2016) 'Northampton's Paralympic champ Ellie Robinson among youngest-ever MBE recipients', Northampton Chronicle Millington, Alison (07/04/2017) 'The insane life of 12-year-old maverick Jenk Oz — Britain's youngest CEO who mingles with Idris Elba, records music, and acts in West End shows', Business Insider
The Church of Scotland (07/17/2017) 'Teenage Glasgow volunteer wins international award'
GfK (05/2017) 'Attitudes around materialism: Global GfK survey', GfK, 2017
United Nations (06/21/2017) 'World population projected to reach 9.8 billion in 2050, and 11.2 billion in 2100', Department of Economic and Social Affairs, United Nations 2017

Printed and bound in Uruguay

2024
34